POLITICAL IDEOLOGY
AND SOCIAL WORK

POLITICAL IDEOLOGY
AND SOCIAL WORK

POLITICAL IDEOLOGY
AND SOCIAL WORK

MITCHELL ROSENWALD

Columbia University Press

New York

Columbia University Press
Publishers Since 1893
New York   Chichester, West Sussex
cup.columbia.edu

Copyright © 2023 Columbia University Press
All rights reserved

Library of Congress Cataloging-in-Publication Data
Names: Rosenwald, Mitchell, author.
Title: Political ideology and social work / Mitchell Rosenwald.
Description: New York : Columbia University Press, 2023. |
Includes bibliographical references and index.
Identifiers: LCCN 2022057767 | ISBN 9780231177429 (hardback) |
ISBN 9780231177436 (trade paperback) |
ISBN 9780231559096 (ebook)
Subjects: LCSH: Social service—Political aspects. | Social workers.
Classification: LCC HV40 .R674 2023 |
DDC 361.3—dc23/eng/20230513
LC record available at https://lccn.loc.gov/2022057767

Printed and bound by CPI Group (UK) Ltd, Croydon, CR0 4YY

Cover design: Noah Arlow

CONTENTS

Foreword   *vii*

Preface   *xi*

1   The Landscape of Political Diversity and
Social Work   1

2   The Evolution of the Profession in Political Context   33

3   Research on Political Diversity and Social Work   61

4   Social Work Education and Political Diversity   87

5   Political Ideology and Social Work Practice   113

6   A Model for Reconciling Political Diversity Among Social
Workers   142

7   Revisiting the Landscape of Political Diversity in
Social Work   152

Epilogue   189

*Appendix: Sample Syllabus on Political Diversity
and Social Work*   *193*

Acknowledgments   *203*

Notes   *205*

References   *207*

Index   *219*

FOREWORD

AMANDA SMITH BARUSCH

THE STARK polarization of American politics has corroded civic life in this country, reaching into families and schools to introduce conflict, damage relationships, and degrade our discourse. Social work classrooms are not insulated from these effects. I encountered them ever more frequently during my three decades as a social work educator. Most recently, when I was director of an MSW program, faculty and I found that maintaining a healthy learning environment was seriously complicated by conflicts that stemmed from intolerance of diverse political views. In a state like Utah, where universities are legally constrained from prohibiting guns on campus, these conflicts could take on a potentially lethal charge.

So, I am delighted to see this book arrive on the scene to offer both hope and practical guidance for addressing these tensions. Mitchell Rosenwald has devoted at least 18 years to the study of political ideologies and social work. Along the way,

FOREWORD

he and I have lately enjoyed an extensive correspondence about healing historical trauma. Rosenwald brings passion, depth, and creativity to his scholarship. The result is this engaging and illuminating book.

The work opens with a clear-headed description of various political ideologies. Rosenwald unpacks the associated beliefs, emphasizing divergent views on the proper role of government, the rights of individuals, and the definition of social justice. He then turns to specific policy issues, using a compendium issued by the NASW Delegate Assembly called *Social Work Speaks* to ground the discussion. By parsing loaded labels like "reactionary" and "progressive" into their component beliefs and practical implications, this work forces us to move beyond stereotypes and begin meaningful discussion of diverse views.

Rosenwald's solid grasp of the dynamics of social work practice comes through as he examines the role that political transference and countertransference can play in the interactions between social workers and clients. His review of research on political ideology underscores its potential influence on both interpersonal dynamics and practice decisions.

Rosenwald's history of the profession brings forth some fascinating details even as it complicates our understanding of the political ideologies that drove social work pioneers. I was intrigued to learn of the role funding might have played in pushing Community Organization Societies (COS) toward more conservative ideologies. The COS and Settlement House movements were influenced by both conservative and liberal perspectives. As Rosenwald puts it, "even with the historic

FOREWORD

backdrop of the profession, political ideology was neither simplistic nor monolithic."

Rosenwald's argument underscores the pervasive tension between the concept of self-determination and the commitment to social justice. To the extent that we emphasize free will, we hold clients responsible for their situations; but social and environmental causes at the macro level cannot be ignored. This insight offers an evocative gateway to explore the implications of diverse political beliefs.

The *piece de resistance* is the closing chapter which reaffirms a commitment to social justice as central to social work practice. Rosenwald pushes back against stereotypes that grind social workers down to bleeding heart liberals, ignoring the depth and diversity of the profession. He offers practical strategies for embracing political diversity in the classroom, drawing from two key intellectual streams. The first, Elizabeth A. Segal's Social Empathy Framework, underscores the important role empathy can play in teaching about social justice. Rosenwald expands on this by introducing techniques from an Intergroup Dialogue model with roots in Paulo Freire's *Pedagogy of the Oppressed.*

As I read *Political Diversity and Social Work*, I was reminded of another book: *Borders and Belonging*, by the Irish poet Pádraig Ó. Tuama. Like Rosenwald, he urges us to redraw stereotypes and to build bridges across difference. With funding from the Irish government's Fund for Reconciliation, Tuama facilitated a series of intense dialogues about Brexit between Irish and English residents with radically opposing political views. Each conversation began with a carefully developed structure. Participants from alternating positions took turns

■ ix ■

FOREWORD

sharing a personal experience of pain or of privilege. This story-based structure offers another rich layer of connection to the important methods found in this book. The insights and understandings generated through both of these promising approaches point the way toward the peace and reconciliation we so desperately need.

PREFACE

AT THE time of this writing, the United States, and indeed, much of the world, is increasingly polarized by political division. While sharp rhetoric has always accompanied politics and policy, the temperature of the rhetoric continues to boil at higher and higher degrees. We do not need to look far for examples.

The challenge to the 2020 transition of power, the insurrection at the Capitol, and the resulting tension, still remains with us today. The Supreme Court's *Dobbs v. Jackson Women's Health Organization* decision—controversial for many and welcomed by others—overturned *Roe v. Wade* and ignited passions and tempers on both sides of the abortion issue. States engaged in inflammatory rhetoric regarding sending immigrants from red states to blue states. Such polarization is unhealthy, of course, and becomes dangerous as rhetoric leads to acts of incivility and outright violence. We are trusting the "other side" (read: those

PREFACE

who disagree with us) less and less. Mistrust and vitriol have replaced respectful disagreement.

Given this context, this book was written not only to examine the contours of political diversity in social work but to provide a measure of calm in the rhetoric. My intention for writing this book is for the social work profession, and all who proudly claim it, to accept that political diversity exists in our profession and to rationally walk a path forward characterized by civil discourse on political views and social justice. Then, the profession can be a vanguard example to "civil society" by charting such a path. Let us begin.

POLITICAL IDEOLOGY
AND SOCIAL WORK

POLITICAL IDEOLOGY
AND SOCIAL WORK

Chapter One

THE LANDSCAPE OF POLITICAL DIVERSITY AND SOCIAL WORK

CONSIDER A social worker who is providing counseling to a same-sex couple who are thinking about getting married. The social worker is not that comfortable with lesbian and gay marriage. She is not sure how to counsel the couple.

Consider a social worker who provides case management to families in the child welfare system. The social worker identifies a viable caregiver for a child who needs one but then learns that the caregiver is undocumented. The social worker supports immigration reform but knows that under current law, the caregiver could be deported. The social worker is not sure whether to support this caregiver as a candidate.

Consider a social work student who is learning in her Social Welfare Policy course that the National Association of Social Workers (NASW) supports women's right to choose. This view runs counter to the student's pro-life views from her Catholic background. She wants to practice with families but

THE LANDSCAPE OF POLITICAL DIVERSITY

is not sure how she would handle a client who is considering abortion.

Consider a social work educator who believes that the profession has become too complacent in supporting existing social institutions instead of radicalizing them. He wants to teach his radical views in a human behavior course but is not sure if that would jeopardize his teaching career.

Consider a social worker who is helping a financially needy client determine if he has sufficient finances. The client earns only $500 more than the ceiling eligibility for the Temporary Aid for Needy Families (TANF) program. The social worker really wants to help this client but is not sure what to do.

Consider a social worker who works in hospice. She strongly believes in physician-assisted suicide (PAS) and works in a state where this policy is legal. One of her patients is in enormous pain and is wondering if PAS is the right route to take. The social worker is struggling with her role in this decision.

Immigration reform. Abortion. Economic assistance for the needy. Same-sex marriage. Political issues routinely dominate the news, and they also routinely arise in the social work profession. Social workers cannot escape the influence or impact of politics in their educational or professional lives. Social workers in healthcare settings routinely face end-of-life care dilemmas. Those employed by community-based clinics intervene with families in which reproductive planning is commonplace. Social workers interact with people using financial assistance programs such as TANF, Social Security Disability Insurance, Housing Choice Vouchers, and the Supplemental Nutritional Assistance Program. They also engage with a full range of clients of various

THE LANDSCAPE OF POLITICAL DIVERSITY

races, gender identities, sexual orientations, and legal statuses. Their views on end-of-life care, family planning, immigration, welfare benefits, and diversity (including issues such as prejudice and discrimination) matter as they impact practice (Rosenwald & Hyde, 2006).

What do all of these issues have in common? They relate to social workers' political views, attitudes, and ideologies. In addition, the diverse range of political ideologies these professionals hold need to be reconciled with the profession at large (Rosenwald, 2006a).

POLITICAL DIVERSITY: CONCEPTUAL FRAMEWORK

The word *political* references how decisions based on policy are made (O'Connors & Sabato, 2000). Cohen (2008) writes, "The origins of the word 'political' itself come . . . from Ancient Greece: *politikos*, pertaining to the running of the city, or polis. In this sense, political philosophy is concerned with the very practical matters of administration" (Cohen, 2008, p. 1) and that "'political philosophy' . . . [is] . . . concerned with fundamental questions about equality, needs and interests, welfare, and human nature" (Cohen, 2008, p. 2).

For millennia, individuals have debated the appropriate structure of the polity and the role of government with regards to its moral obligation in providing social welfare to its citizens (Cohen, 2008). Rousseau's *The Discourse on Inequality* and *The Social Contract* helped formulate the responsibility government

▪ 3 ▪

THE LANDSCAPE OF POLITICAL DIVERSITY

has to its citizenry as a matter of public policy (Cohen, 2008). In the spirit of democracy, "a citizenry [should have] the ability to convert its views on the issues of the day—certainly the pressing, salient issues—into public policy" (Maisel & Brewer, 2010, p. 11). But factors such as the direction of policy change (progressive or regressive), the speed of change, and the depth of change all shape the decisions of public policy (Baradat & Phillips, 2020). It is only through this messy mechanism of politics that government leaders can establish public policy that approaches current standards of rights, justice, and equality. Of course, these standards can counter each other. And so the question remains: What is the *right* role of government in creating policy, and in what policies—and to what extent—should government intervene?

Political ideology is grounded in overarching sets of values of that prescribe the interplay between the individual and government (Abbott, 1988; Cohen, 2008; Koeske & Crouse, 1981; Lowi & Ginsberg, 1994; McKenna, 1998). Framing the context in which policy formation occurs, Wertheimer (2002) writes, "At the most basic level, the problem is this. We believe that the individual is the primary locus of moral value and that individual freedom is of the utmost importance. At the same time, we think that the state is justified in using its coercive powers to limit individual liberty if it does so for the right reasons. Unfortunately, we disagree as to what those reasons are" (p. 38). "Political ideologies help people make sense of the world and can help people understand the various policy options available to governments" (Rom, Hidaka, & Walker, 2022, p. 93). In sum, political ideology is defined by those values that relate

THE LANDSCAPE OF POLITICAL DIVERSITY

to positions on public policy. In this book, we will explore the political ideologies of social workers; we will refer to the range of ideologies we encounter as social workers' *political diversity.* We will be interested in the full range and content of this political diversity as it relates to social work practice.

For the purposes of discussion, *political diversity* can be defined as the range of ideologies or beliefs that individual social workers espouse on public policy issues (Rosenwald, 2006a). These issues constitute a whole range of operationalized political thought, and for social work they are manifested in *Social Work Speaks* (National Association of Social Workers, 2021b), the peer-reviewed and recognized "gold standard" of the social work profession. It provides position statements on a variety of social policies voted on by NASW's Delegate Assembly every three years (National Association of Social Workers, 2021b). This compendium of public policy positions includes dozens of policy statements that "represent" social work, including abortion; racism; welfare reform; lesbian, gay, and bisexual issues; community development; transgender and gender identity issues; and end-of-life care (National Association of Social Workers, 2021b). This publication is an important reflection of the official positions of the profession because NASW is the largest professional social work organization in the world, represents some 120,000 members, and sets policy and practice guidelines for the profession at large (National Association of Social Workers, 2021b). Ranging from the profession's statements on affirmative action and genetics to family planning and reproductive choice, and to civil liberties and justice, these policy positions anchor the profession's value

■ 5 ■

base and frame the direction for practice and research. Abbott (1988) used these statements as the basis of her much-cited Professional Opinion Scale, which examined social workers' values; the scale gauges political ideologies as it was created from these policy statements (Rosenwald, 2006a).

POLITICAL PHILOSOPHIES AND THE RANGE OF POLITICAL IDEOLOGY DIVERSITY

The political ideologies discussed in this book are embedded in political philosophies (Rom, Hidaka, & Walker, 2022). Democratic liberalism was born in the twentieth century and reflects a focus on capitalism, individual rights, equality, and voter participation (Rom, Hidaka, & Walker, 2022). Libertarianism focuses on individuals' rights and privacy with very limited government regulation (including of income) (Brennan, 2016; Rom, Hidaka, & Walker, 2022). Social conservatism subscribes to the government maintaining traditional morals held over generations. Socialism is the belief in the need for a heavy reliance on government responsibility in ensuring equality and is aligned with structural critiques, including environmentalism and critical race theory and the diversity, equity, and inclusion movement (Rom, Hidaka, & Walker, 2022; see also Brennan, 2016). This latter movement is called the "New Left" and is associated with progressive ideology. In contrast, the "New Right" is associated with the importance of tradition and religious creed in shaping social policy. This ideology

THE LANDSCAPE OF POLITICAL DIVERSITY

is also aligned with conservative populism, which focuses on "the need to win elections in order to install a government that will respond to the demands of ordinary people" (Rom, Hidaka, & Walker, 2022, p. 94).

Political diversity includes a spectrum of political ideologies that will be defined using the familiar range of conservative–liberal ideology noted by a number of scholars (Baradat & Philips, 2020; Karger & Stoez, 2018; Knight, 1999: Lowi & Ginsberg, 2002). Baradat and Phillips (2020) delineate five types in a spectrum that reflect a politically ideological range—radical, liberal, moderate, conservative, and reactionary. Rom, Hidaka, and Walker (2022) use "New Right" to reference "reactionary," and this term will be used in the continuum as the term is more neutral, and less pejorative. "New Left" or "Progressive" is often used to reflect ideologies very left of center (Rom, Hidaka, & Walker, 2022). While these conceptual meanings can change (Baradat & Phillips, 2020; McKenna, 1998), in this book, the contemporary meanings will be used.

As with any spectrum, these five components are useful to illustrate general concepts yet vary from individual to individual. Furthermore, while these types are explanatory, the degree to which individuals identify with a particular term probably varies. Figure 1.1 depicts this spectrum.

FIGURE 1.1 Spectrum of political ideology.

THE LANDSCAPE OF POLITICAL DIVERSITY

"NEW LEFT" IDEOLOGY

The first type of ideology—New Left ideology, also known currently as Progressive ideology—reflects those individuals who most strongly want fundamental change to society by replacing oppressive institutions with more equitable ones. "They reject the institutions of the establishment, calling for a more human, egalitarian, and idealistic social and political system" (Baradat & Phillips, 2020, p. 19). From critiques of capitalism as a form of economic production and distribution to the military as an institution that wars, at the extreme, those who hold these views believe that society would be better organized with fairer systems, such as socialism, that value equity over competition and cooperation over domination (Rom, Hidaka, & Walker, 2022). Social change should occur on a grand scale; its speed should be swift.[1]

Historically, this ideology draws from three sources (Longres, 1996). Revolutionary Marxists hold the most radical perspective, believing capitalism is the foundation for explaining oppression (Longres). Evolutionary Marxists, while citing the primacy of class conflict, attribute other types of conflict to the problems that the working class experience. (Longres). Social Democrats are the least radical of the three and treat capitalism as one cause, of a myriad, of oppression (Longres). Therefore, the reach of capitalism in causing distress varies by each of the three perspectives.

New Left ideology is also influenced by feminism that seeks social reorganization to free women from the subordination of male domination (Wagner, 1990) and all marginalized groups from oppressive systems. Moreover, it relies on the New Left's

THE LANDSCAPE OF POLITICAL DIVERSITY

foci "[as] a vanguard for social change, in decentralized authority and local control, and in participatory democracy and skepticism about Leninist parties" (Wagner, 1990, p. 62). The New Left believes liberal ideology reflected in the "center left" is "insufficiently progressive" and society as a whole ignores the New Left's ideas (Rom, Hidaka, & Walker, 2022, pp. 92–93).

"LIBERAL" IDEOLOGY

The second ideology—liberal ideology—recognizes that social inequities exist and seeks to ensure that everyone has a "fair" chance in achieving opportunities. "Liberals . . . generally appreciate the concept of the law, and although they may want to change certain specifics of it, they will usually not violate it to accomplish their political objectives" (Baradat & Phillips, 2020, p. 201). This ideology has roots in Democratic liberalism (see Rom, Hidaka, & Walker, 2022).

Liberal ideology favors governmental protection of individual rights (Dolgoff & Feldstein, 2003; Lowi & Ginsberg, 2002) and strongly believes in the government's mission to protect those citizens who experience disenfranchisement and powerlessness (O'Connors & Sabato, 2000). In fact, government is the only true "safety net" to help those in need when private charity is absent or not sufficient in scope (Sargent, 1995). Therefore, fully funding government entitlement programs such as Housing Choice Vouchers ("Section 8"), Supplemental Nutritional Assistance Program ("food stamps"), and Medical Assistance, as well as raising the minimum wage to a living wage, are essential to those who are liberal. Further, liberal views include the

THE LANDSCAPE OF POLITICAL DIVERSITY

separation of religion and politics ("church and state") (Brint, 1994; McKenna, 1998) and rationally motivated change within existing institutions (Baradat & Phillips, 2020, Sargent, 1995).

"MODERATE" IDEOLOGY

The third political ideology—moderate ideology—relies on an appreciation of perspectives from the left and the right. Although moderatism has no "philosophical foundation," its existence reflects the reality that individuals hold mildly strong political cal views on a range of issues (Baradat & Phillips, 2020, p. 22). "Moderates are fundamentally satisfied with the society, although they agree there is room for improvement and recognize several specific areas in need of modification" (p. 22). Moderates favor gradual over disruptive change (Baradat & Phillips, 2020, p. 22)

Moderates subscribe to liberal *and* conservative views based on the nature of the issue (Berman & Murphy, 2012; McKenna, 1998). For example, an individual with a moderate ideology could support both a woman's right to have an abortion (a more liberal value) and the importance of deregulating government (a more conservative value) (Berman & Murphy, 1999). This ideology values "caution and consistency" and argues for planned, incremental change (McKenna, 1998).

"CONSERVATIVE" IDEOLOGY

The fourth ideology—conservative ideology—questions the scope and process of social change and most closely favors the status quo (Baradat & Phillips, 2020). This ideology opposes

THE LANDSCAPE OF POLITICAL DIVERSITY

change due to a skepticism that improvement can occur through government (Baradat & Phillips; Dolgoff & Feldstein, 2003; O'Connors & Sabato, 2000). This social conservatism aligns somewhat with libertarianism, though libertarianism's support for same-sex relationships and marijuana legalization conflicts with the tenets of social conservatism (see Rom, Hidaka, & Walker, 2022).

A conservative ideology prioritizes voluntary and for-profit sectors' roles in helping alleviate people's suffering (Dolgoff & Feldstein, 2003; O'Connors & Sabato, 2000). This ideology protects individual rights from government incursion, supports traditional values (e.g., pro-life stance, anti-same-sex marriage), and advocates for lower taxes (Lowi & Ginsberg, 2002; Sargent, 1995). Tenets include the primacy of individual freedom's centrality and suspicion that government can entrap individuals into cycles of dependency (Sargent, 1995). Finally, conservative ideology posits any social change should occur slowly (Baradat & Phillips, 2020; Sargent, 1995).

"NEW RIGHT" IDEOLOGY

The fifth ideology—New Right ideology—is dissatisfied with the status quo and favors a return to values and policies of yesteryear. "[Referencing this reactionary ideology] all reactionaries reject claims to human equality and favor distributing wealth unequally" (Baradat & Phillips, 2020, p. 32). Furthermore, those who are New Right "reject notions of social progress . . . and look backward to previously held norms or values" (Baradat & Phillips, 2020, p. 32).

THE LANDSCAPE OF POLITICAL DIVERSITY

Historically, the New Right ideology is represented by several segments that at times overlap. The New Christian Right (including the Christian Identity Movement) is a movement associated with biblical literalism and includes promoting prayer in school, banning abortion, repealing laws that protect lesbian, gay, bisexual, and transgender (LGBT) individuals, censoring offensive content in the media, and advocating for tax breaks for Christian-based schools (Baradat & Phillips, 2020; Berlet, 1995; Diamond, 1989; Hyde, 1991). The secular New Right champions the capitalist system, for moral reasons as well as economic ones, and believes capitalism ultimately flourishes when women "tame" men to be more responsible in the context of marriage (Hyde, 1991; Rosenwald, 2004). Finally, the "pro-family" segment of the New Right advocates for the return of patriarchal family roles (husbands employed full-time while wives raise children full-time); ending abortion, preventing LGBT rights, and ensuring the Equal Rights Amendment never passed (which it did not) (Hyde, 1991; see also Rom, Hidaka, & Walker, 2022). Those in the New Right are concerned "that the culture has been weaponized against all they hold dear" (Rom, Hidaka, & Walker, p. 93).

COMPLEXITY OF POLITICAL DIVERSITY

While this description of the five ideal types of political ideology delineates the political diversity or range of ideologies to which individuals may subscribe, it can oversimplify the reality of what people actually believe. Human beings are complex, and they are rarely monolithic on every issue with respect to political

THE LANDSCAPE OF POLITICAL DIVERSITY

ideology. Therefore, it is helpful to strengthen the political ideology's validity by distinguishing its "social" and "economic" components (Lowi & Ginsberg, 2002). Brint (1994; see also McKenna, 1998) distinguishes economic issues into issues of "egalitarian and basic system commitment" [e.g., support for capitalism] and "welfare state [e.g., income assistance for the poor]." Similarly, Brint (1994) divides social issues into several subcategories. Individualism and social equality issues are represented, respectively, by "civil liberties" [e.g., First Amendment related issues], civil rights" [e.g., equity for all groups] and "morality" – including "military." Table 1.1 presents a spectrum of political diversity (Baradat & Phillips, 2020) delineated by the specific components of political ideologies (Brint, 1994). Here we can see a more comprehensive—and nuanced—composite of an individual's political ideology.

We can organize *Social Work Speaks*'s "Policy Statement Topic Areas" (National Association of Social Workers, 2021b) by Brint's (1994) framework; they appear in table 1.2. Each topic area is detailed in a "Public and Professional Policy Statement" (National Association of Social Workers, 2018). Please note that the organization of the policy statements is based first on the author's view of where they might fit—into basic system commitment, welfare reform, civil rights issue, or morality issue per Brint's (1994) framework. For example, the issue of physical punishment of children relates to both the morality of physical punishment as well as the civil rights of a child. There will surely be overlap between some, if not all, of the statements, but this at least provides us with an initial framework to organize the particular policies. Also, while there are sixty-two statements, six

■ 13 ■

TABLE 1.1 Spectrum of Political Ideology by Economic and Social Components

Component	New Left/ Progressive	Liberal	Moderate	Conservative	New Right
Economic: Egalitarian and Basic System Commitment (Support for Capitalism)	Capitalism is illusory for giving everyone "equal opportunity." Idea of Weber's "life chances" (not everyone starts at the same place on the "starting line.") Role of government is to ensure that everyone has true equal access to means of production—socialism and communism are more ideal economic systems than capitalism.	Capitalism has major flaws and government needs to assist those who are disadvantaged by capitalism to ensure that everyone has as fair a chance as possible.	Capitalism basically works well as a system though it needs some minor adjustments.	Capitalism works quite well. Individual competition is the bedrock of the economy. Very minor adjustments needed for class inequity. Supply-side economics.	Capitalism is vital to economic growth. Patriarchy and capitalism work well together.

Economic: Welfare State	Capitalism inherently breeds massive inequality. Providing public assistance is important but only serves as a "band-aid" and further perpetuates a dysfunctional system. Permanent underclass and real lack of social (class) mobility.	Public sector should take the lead in providing key welfare programs to alleviate human suffering (housing, food, financial assistance, and energy assistance) as well as champion living wage initiatives.	A combination of private and public sectors provides the best assistance to help those in emergency need.	Private sector (for-profit, nonprofit, and sectarian groups) can more efficiently assist individuals in emergency economic distress. "Pull yourself up by your bootstraps" adage. Protestant work ethic and rugged individualism. Government-based, nonemergency welfare rarely necessary.	Religious groups are particularly poised to provide assistance to those in need. Opposed to most government welfare (with some exceptions—Social Security, military)

(continued)

TABLE 1.1 (*Continued*)

Component	New Left/ Progressive	Liberal	Moderate	Conservative	New Right
Social: Civil Rights	Patriarchal, capitalism-based government perpetuates human inequity. At the minimum, government is vital to redressing those social inequities born from a group's histories and present experiences with oppression but experiences of oppression will occur with maintenance of current economic and political structure.	Government has a strong role to play in legally redressing enduring housing, employment, criminal justice, and relationship inequities among repressed groups (women, LGBTQ, people of color, seniors, individuals with disabilities, prisoners).	Government has some role to play in addressing past and present inequities though some claims of oppression are overstated or nonexistent.	Government has a very limited role in addressing civil rights issues as they have largely been addressed in the past. Generally opposed to affirmative action.	Government has no role in addressing civil rights issues—consider them "special rights."

Social: Morality and Military Force	Military intervention only provides illusory temporary fixes but does not resolve long-standing problems. Real change occurs through nonviolent social action. Morality—Individuals have absolute choice in governing their bodies whether it relates to bringing children into the world, testing a fetus for any potential genetic "challenge," or deciding when to end life. Pro-choice and assisted suicide. Anti-death penalty.	Military has an essential role to play in protecting the United States though more "dovish" on use of force. Morality—Individuals have absolute choice in governing their bodies whether it relates to bringing children into the world, testing a fetus for any potential genetic "challenge," or deciding when to end life. Pro-choice and assisted suicide. Anti-death penalty.	Military might should be considered when U.S. interests are at stake. Morality—Individuals have some choice in governing bodies relating to abortion and ending life (assisted suicide). Anti- or pro-death penalty.	Military might is a lead source of resolving conflict to protect U.S. interests. Morality—Individuals have no choice in governing bodies relating to abortion (except when the mother's health is at risk) and ending life. Pro-death penalty.	Military might is core to the United States' standing in world. Libertarian view is military might should be used only for defense of the homeland. Morality—Pro-life and anti-contraception. Preserve life with "all means necessary." Individuals have an absolute right to protect their bodies' integrity from government-mandated vaccines. Pro-death penalty.

Source: Contributions from Baradat and Phillips (2020) and Brint (1994).

Note: Brint's (1994) subcomponent of social issues—civil liberties—is removed from the typology as subsequent *Social Work Speaks* issues are not viewed by this author as relevant to this dimension of political ideology.

THE LANDSCAPE OF POLITICAL DIVERSITY

of them did not seem relevant to political diversity per se (e.g., Technology and Social Work, and Professional Self-Care and Social Work did not seem to have a political dimension). These six statements are excluded from the table. As a result, those that remain are what this author deemed relevant to Brint's (1994) framework. (For example, all policy topics relating to creating and ending life [i.e., Genetics, Reproductive Justice, End-of-Life Decision Making and Care, Capital Punishment and the Death Penalty] are placed under "Morality," as Brint [1994] categorized life-related policies in this way.)

Some policies did not fit neatly into any of Brint's (1994) conception based on this author's assessment; therefore, they are placed under new subcategories of "Social" (though recognizing welfare state components of all of them as they rely on funding streams). These new categories include five policies under "Child Welfare" (e.g., Foster Care and Adoption); three policies under "Education" (e.g., School Safety); and five categories under "Health" (e.g., Long-Term Services and Support). Three remaining items could not be located in other subcategories and were placed in an "Other" subcategory under "Social."

Note that the fifty-six policy positions listed in table 1.2 might vary in their relevance to actual social work practice based on a practitioner's particular workplace and area of expertise. That is, a social worker in the foster care system might have an opinion on capital punishment though never apply this view in practice. Therefore, when conceptualizing political diversity among social workers, we can think of their general attitudes toward an array of policies as well as a smaller catchment of policies relevant to their actual practice.

TABLE 1.2 Social Work Policy Positions by Economic and Social Components of Political Ideology and Spectrum of Political Diversity

Political Ideology Component	Policy Statement Topic Areas
Economic: Egalitarian and Basic System Commitment	• Economic Justice • Role of Government, Social Policy, and Social Work
Economic: Welfare State	• Community Development • Environmental Policy • Family Policy • Health Care • Homelessness • Housing • Social Services • Welfare Reform • Affirmative Action
Social: Civil Rights	• Civil Liberties and Social Justice • Cultural and Linguistic Competence in the Social Work Profession • Crime Victim Assistance • HIV and AIDS • Human Trafficking • Immigrants and Refugees • International Policy on Human Rights • Juvenile Justice and Delinquency Prevention • Language Diversity in the United States • Lesbian, Gay, and Bisexual Issues • Mental Health • People with Disabilities • Sex Trade and Social Work Practice • Racism • Social Work in the Criminal Justice System • Sovereignty, Rights, and the Well-Being of Indigenous Peoples Living in the United States

(continued)

TABLE 1.2 *(Continued)*

Political Ideology Component	Policy Statement Topic Areas
	• Transgender and Gender-Nonconforming People • Voter Rights and Voter Participation • Women in the Social Work Profession • Women's Issues • Workplace Discrimination
Social: Morality and Military Force	**Morality** • Adolescent Pregnancy and Parenting • Capital Punishment and the Death Penalty • End-of-Life Decision Making and Care • Genetics • Hospice Care • Reproductive Justice **Military Force** • Peace and Social Justice
Social: Child Welfare	• Child Abuse and Neglect • Child Welfare Workforce • Family Violence • Foster Care and Adoption • Parental Abduction
Social: Education	• Early Childhood Care and Services • Education of Children and Adolescents • School Safety
Social: Health	• Adolescent and Young Adult Health • Aging and Wellness • Disasters • Long-Term Services and Supports • Substance Use Disorder Treatment • Youth Suicide
Social: Other	• Electoral Politics • Employee Assistance • Rural Social Work

Source: "Policy Statement Topic Areas" from *Social Work Speaks*, National Association of Social Workers (2021b).

THE LANDSCAPE OF POLITICAL DIVERSITY

Furthermore, social workers' views on a particular policy statement might vary quite little with respect to their political diversity depending on how polarizing the issues are. For example, social workers' political views on the civil rights of prisoners might range much more dramatically than their political views on public child welfare. On this note, we can conceptualize that the additional constructions of child welfare, education, and health relate to welfare state issues with respect to public vs. private service delivery as well as the extent that public expenditures should be appropriated to resolving these policy areas.[2]

To capture other salient policy positions forwarded by *Social Work Speaks*, other subcategories were created within "Social": "Child Welfare," "Education," "Health," and "Other."

From table 1.2, within the spectrum of political diversity, we can understand more fully its economic and social components and how the profession's policies can be organized by such a framework. Political diversity is a complex variable worthy of discussion and study in social work though its presence has been largely ignored.

Note that the content of this book is the political context of the United States. Political ideology and political movements can look quite different in other nations (Abbott, 1999).

WHERE HAS THE CONVERSATION ON POLITICAL DIVERSITY BEEN?

The most casual glance at social work literature over the past three decades shows the proliferation of the profession's commitment

THE LANDSCAPE OF POLITICAL DIVERSITY

to developing diversity knowledge on race and ethnicity, sexual orientation, gender, gender identity, ability, age, class, national origin, and immigration status. Books focusing on diversity as a cornerstone of social work practice first appeared in the 1990s and continue in the present (e.g., Anderson & Carter, 2002; Harrison, Wodarski, & Thyer, 1992; Marsiglia & Kulis, 2016). The profession places major emphasis on the principles of diversity and generates scholarship on the application of diversity ranging from social work education (Van Soest & Garcia, 2008) to ethics (National Association of Social Workers, 2021a) and policy (National Association of Social Workers, 2021c).

Yet unlike the rich scholarship on such diversity variables, political diversity, as a diversity variable, has historically been neglected as an area of focus (Epstein, 2011; Galambos, 2009; Rosenwald, 2006a). The social work profession has remained largely silent on this topic.

One can argue that in the social work profession, those of varying or perhaps unpopular political viewpoints have not shared similar histories of oppression, such as those of minority race, ethnicity, religious beliefs, or sexual orientation have faced. This is largely true. As social workers in the United States, we work much more with individuals who have experienced oppression associated with racism, sexism, and homophobia rather than political oppression. Concomitantly, it is more likely that from a practice perspective, one's countertransference, that is, the feelings brought up in a social worker when interacting with a client, is more rooted in feelings of race, class, and age than of working with a client whose political orientation is different.

Additionally, consider the necessity of a history of oppression in the inclusion of a diversity variable—perhaps it is necessary to have an oppressive history to accord a variable diversity status. The oppression of a conservative—or of a progressive—in the United States and in social work does not at all match, and perhaps it may be absent from the very real discriminatory histories that others have faced (e.g., those with [dis]abilities or the LGBTQ population). Yet while oppression might be absent, prejudice may still occur for those both on the right and the left of mainstream (liberal) social work. Because those with progressive or New Left ideologies have not encountered a contemporary history of oppression in the United States, that might explain why it has not received much focus and why it is called a "barely audible conversation on political ideology in social work" (Rosenwald, 2006, p. 121).[3]

Another reason this discussion might not occur is that it is a bit of a taboo topic in social work. As will be discussed further, there is an explicit statement, and there is certainly an implicit assumption, that the social work profession espouses a liberal ideology. It certainly seems to, when one examines the policy statements of *Social Work Speaks* (National Association of Social Workers, 2021b) and compares them to the Democratic Party's policy platform (Democratic National Committee, 2020) as opposed to that of the Republican Party (Republican National Committee, 2021). Those who espouse political views that are not liberal or outside of mainstream social work might feel closeted and stigmatized.

In any event, regardless of conjectures about the relative weight of political diversity as compared to other diversity variables—or the taboo nature of this line of inquiry—a number of rationales necessitate political diversity's inclusion in social work as a variable worthy of inquiry and scholarship.

RATIONALES FOR EXPLORING POLITICAL DIVERSITY IN SOCIAL WORK

In canvassing the landscape as to the near absence of discussion of political diversity in social work to the extent of other diversity variables, we can identify a number of rationales for elevating it to an area of attention, discussion, and study in social work.

One reason relates to social work accreditation standards. "Political ideology" is listed in the diversity statement of the Educational Policy and Accreditation Standards that the Council on Social Work Education (CSWE) uses to evaluate BSW and MSW programs (Council on Social Work Education, 2022). Interestingly, political ideology was absent from the diversity statement in CSWE's accreditation standards prior to 2008—an omission that is at least curious and suggests that it was not seen as important before. Social work educational programs need to know much more about how it is conceptualized and operationalized (Epstein, 2011; Galambos, 2009). Galambos (2009) states that, generally, the social work profession honors tolerance but questions if "we stand up to this definition in

THE LANDSCAPE OF POLITICAL DIVERSITY

our treatment of differences in political ideology? Maybe not" (p. 343). She continues: "If we believe that education can influence opinions, values, world views, and professional conduct, then implementing a true deliberative classroom environment can be a more effective method for embracing political tolerance. Viewing political tolerance as an acceptable value of democratic societies can lead to a better understanding of political diversity in social work" (Galambos, p. 346).

Some educators even question if social work educators act as bullies by indoctrinating social work students into a liberal ideology (Flaherty et al., 2013). Rosenwald et al. (2012) offer an initial way to consider a framework and strategies to address political conversations in the classroom.

The second reason to address political diversity relates to the profession's ethical code. "Political belief" is listed in the NASW *Code of Ethics* (National Association of Social Workers, 2021a) as a diversity component that social workers should learn about, understand, and respect (see Section 1.05, Cultural Competence and Social Diversity): "(c) Social workers should obtain education about and seek to understand the nature of social diversity and oppression with respect to race, ethnicity, national origin, color, sex, sexual orientation, gender identity or expression, age, marital status, political belief, religion, immigration status, and mental or physical disability" (National Association of Social Workers, 2021a). After engaging in an extensive review of different professional codes of ethics, Buila (2010) argues that social workers "with a progressive worldview may feel a better fit with the profession of social work" due to an allegiance with the *Code of Ethics*, though she also states the profession should

■ 25 ■

not exclude anyone based on "orthodox" or "conservative" political ideology (Buila, p. 6). Kirst-Ashman (2007) writes that "social work values tend to be more liberal than conservative, as is demonstrated by the NASW *Code of Ethics*" (p. 14). Hodge (2014) makes this point and cites that discrimination occurs toward Evangelical Christian social workers though Bolen & Dessel (2013) question the extent of this claim.

The third reason relates to assessing the profession's policy stance. As previously mentioned, *Social Work Speaks* (National Association of Social Workers, 2021b) is a compendium of public policy positions that includes dozens of policy statements for the profession to follow.

While officially nonpartisan, NASW's (2021b) policy positions contained in *Social Work Speaks* align much more closely with those of a liberal ideology (Rosenwald, 2006b) and, as previously mentioned, with the Democratic Party's platform (Democratic National Committee, 2020). This "policy formation dilemma" is addressed in the very position on "Electoral Politics" within *Social Work Speaks* (National Association of Social Workers, 2021b) and can extend broadly to our discussion.

> Social workers frequently approach electoral politics with great caution because of its potential for divisiveness. The major cause for division occurs around the concepts of partisanship and political parties. Some members of the profession believe that NASW should be nonpartisan in terms of candidates for office or that NASW should take positions only on issues, not candidates. Other members think

THE LANDSCAPE OF POLITICAL DIVERSITY

that NASW should be aligned with only one of the major parties, and still others favor a bipartisan approach. . . . NASW can promote inclusion of members in its political activities by respecting the diversity of political positions they hold. (National Association of Social Workers, 2021b, pp. 91, 93)

Forming official policy statements is a real challenge when the profession is so diverse.

A final reason relates to addressing the profession's depiction to the public. This point was most provocatively illustrated in 2007 when columnist George Will, a self-identified conservative and citing the National Association of Scholars, accused the social work profession of indoctrinating students into a "progressive" ideology (this related to several social work education programs requiring certain assignments to social work students). Below is Will's (2007) provocative editorial:

CODE OF COERCION

In 1943, the Supreme Court, affirming the right of Jehovah's Witnesses children to refuse to pledge allegiance to the U.S. flag in schools, declared: "No official, high or petty, can prescribe what shall be orthodox in politics, nationalism, religion or other matters of opinion, or force citizens to confess by word or act their faith therein." Today that principle is routinely traduced, coast to coast, by officials who are petty in several senses.

THE LANDSCAPE OF POLITICAL DIVERSITY

They are teachers at public universities, in schools of social work. A study prepared by the National Association of Scholars, a group that combats political correctness on campuses, reviews social work education programs at 10 major public universities and comes to this conclusion: Such programs mandate an ideological orthodoxy to which students must subscribe concerning "social justice" and "oppression."

In 1997, the National Association of Social Workers (NASW) adopted a surreptitious political agenda in the form of a new code of ethics, enjoining social workers to advocate for social justice "from local to global levels." A widely used textbook—"Direct Social Work Practice: Theory and Skill"—declares that promoting "social and economic justice" is especially imperative as a response to "the conservative trends of the past three decades." Clearly, in the social work profession's catechism, whatever social and economic justice are, they are the opposite of conservatism.

The Council on Social Work Education (CSWE), the national accreditor of social work education programs, encourages—not that encouragement is required—the ideological permeation of the curricula, including mandatory student advocacy. The CSWE says students must demonstrate an ability to "understand the forms and mechanisms of oppression and discrimination."

At Arizona State University, social work students must "demonstrate compliance with the NASW Code of Ethics." Berkeley requires compliance as proof of "suitability for the profession." Students at the University of Central Florida

■ 28 ■

THE LANDSCAPE OF POLITICAL DIVERSITY

"must comply" with the NASW code. At the University of Houston, students must sign a pledge of adherence. At the University of Michigan, failure to comply with the code may be deemed "academic misconduct."

Schools' mission statements, student manuals and course descriptions are clotted with the vocabulary of "progressive" cant—"diversity," "inclusion," "classism," "ethnocentrism," "racism," "sexism," "heterosexism," "ageism," "white privilege," "ableism," "contextualizes subjects," "cultural imperialism," "social identities and positionalities," "biopsychosocial" problems, "a just share of society's resources," and on and on. What goes on under the cover of this miasma of jargon? Just what the American Association of University Professors warned against in its 1915 "Declaration of Principles"— teachers "indoctrinating" students.

In 2005, Emily Brooker, a social-work student at Missouri State University, was enrolled in a class taught by a professor who advertised himself as a liberal and insisted that social work is a liberal profession. At first, a mandatory assignment for his class was to advocate homosexual foster homes and adoption, with all students required to sign an advocacy letter, on university stationery, to the state legislature.

When Brooker objected on religious grounds, the project was made optional. But shortly before the final exam she was charged with a "Level 3," the most serious violation of professional standards. In a 2 1/2-hour hearing—which she was forbidden to record and which her parents were barred from attending—the primary subject was her refusal to sign the letter. She was ordered to write a paper ("Written Response

THE LANDSCAPE OF POLITICAL DIVERSITY

about My Awareness") explaining how she could "lessen the gap" between her ethics and those of the social-work profession. When she sued the university, it dropped the charges and made financial and other restitution.

The NAS study says that at Rhode Island College's School of Social Work, a conservative student, William Felkner, received a failing grade in a course requiring students to lobby the state legislature for a cause mandated by the department. The NAS study also reports that Sandra Fuiten abandoned her pursuit of a social-work degree at the University of Illinois at Springfield after the professor, in a course that required students to lobby the legislature on behalf of positions prescribed by the professor, told her that it is impossible to be both a social worker and an opponent of abortion.

In the month since the NAS released its study, none of the schools covered by it has contested its findings. Because there might as well be signs on the doors of many schools of social work proclaiming "conservatives need not apply," two questions arise: Why are such schools of indoctrination permitted in institutions of higher education? And why are people of all political persuasions taxed to finance this propaganda?

The social work profession was not quiet in its response; the two largest social work organizations responded directly to Will's challenge. The CSWE's education executive director, Julia Watkins (2007), stated social workers should "embrace the profession's historical commitment to social justice [and]

■ 30 ■

THE LANDSCAPE OF POLITICAL DIVERSITY

CSWE will continue its dedication to quality assurance and program expectations that ensure open respectful participation by faculty and students" (para. 4). The NASW's executive director, Betsy Clark (2007), affirmed that "our members hold a diverse array of opinions on social issues. . . . Social workers do not apologize for caring about people marginalized by society, nor do we apologize for holding members of our profession to high standards" (p. A13).

As evident in those two responses, social work leaders reflected an adherence to an important professional value base. In light of both of these organizations' inclusion of the importance of political diversity, the question remains how to negotiate this diversity in light of the "program expectations" and "profession[al] . . . high standards" referenced.

The above rationales provide a number of reasons why political diversity should be legitimized as a variable in the social work profession. Indeed, the profession prides itself on subscribing to principles of diversity that guide its ethical approach, its practice frameworks, and its education standards. Yet one diversity item—political diversity—has not received the same amount of study that other diversity variables have. As a consequence, social work can benefit from an in-depth critique and conceptual exploration of this variable to further strengthen the profession. In the chapters that follow, we will take a look at how the profession's history and political ideological views developed—often in competing directions. We will closely examine how political ideology is realized and managed in both social work education and social work practice. We will explore future directions in research into this topic as well.

■ 31 ■

THE LANDSCAPE OF POLITICAL DIVERSITY

As a profession that is committed to a value base as well as diversity in all forms, a tension exists between honoring political diversity and following through on this promise. How does a value-based profession, as articulated in its policy statements and ethical code, account for those professionals and students who disagree with them? The identification and assessment of political diversity in social work—and the profession's response—in the domains of its historical and emerging identity, professional ethics, education, professional socialization, practice, policy development, and research are vital for the social work profession to address to increase its inclusivity and strengthen its professional unity. This conversation needs to occur.

Chapter Two

THE EVOLUTION OF THE PROFESSION IN POLITICAL CONTEXT

THIS CHAPTER seeks to place the evolution of the profession within the political context of the nation since social work's inception. While the history of the profession is well documented in terms of its social justice and charity roots, and tension with professionalization (e.g., Trattner, 1999; Specht & Courtney, 1994), the explicit lens of the profession through a political ideology lens has not been wholly examined. Therefore, examining the profession's ideological stance through the frame of social welfare centers this chapter. The spectrum of political diversity introduced in chapter 1 is used to assess the profession's response.

The extent of the profession's advocacy and overall response to key social welfare milestones reflects the political ideology of the profession in various eras of social welfare policy in the United States. This professional response is examined in the time period corresponding to the arc of the profession's

THE EVOLUTION OF THE PROFESSION

emergence through present day—from the late 1800s to the early 2020s. To what extent did the profession, through its focus, organization, and activities, serve to agitate and advocate for social welfare reform in these eras? At what points was the profession largely silent or absent from such advocacy? In sum, how did the profession's activities align—or not—with various initiatives of different eras of social welfare policy since its inception?

DOROTHEA DIX AND THE PIERCE ADMINISTRATION

As a starting point, we can begin in the 1850s, a few decades before the formation of the settlement houses and charity organization societies' movements. We look to the early social work advocacy of Dorothea Dix and the response of President Franklin Pierce. Her advocacy foreshadowed the mostly liberal ideology that would galvanize the profession in the settlement houses several decades later.

Dix's celebrity stems from her leadership in providing the first federal response to helping those with mental illness (Ginsberg, 1998). She traversed the nation to raise financial support to help create state asylums and sufficient housing and services for those with mental illness (Ginsberg, 1998). Her and others' advocacy led to Congress's support of ten million acres for the "insane" as well as the federal mandate for service provision for those who were blind and deaf. Despite these efforts and Congressional support, in 1854, President Pierce vetoed the bill: "In

■ 34 ■

THE EVOLUTION OF THE PROFESSION

his veto message he acknowledged the responsibility of citizens to discharge a high and holy duty of providing for those who 'are subject to want and disuse of body or mind.' He concluded, however, that providing such help was not the job of the federal government: "I can not find any authority in the Constitution for making the Federal Government the great almoner of public charity throughout the United States'" (Axinn & Levin, 1992, p. 47, cited in Ginsberg, 1998, p. 22). Expanding on the rationale behind Pierce's veto, Dolgoff and Feldstein (2003) articulate that he perceived helping one group in need would necessitate helping all vulnerable groups; "despite the clause in the preamble of the U. S. Constitution obliging it 'to promote the general welfare,' he did not believe this translated into government assistance (Ginsberg, 1998, p. 22). Here, we see Dix's advocacy for those with psychiatric and physical challenges thwarted by a conservative administration that would set the stage for the social work profession in its initial advocacy efforts.

POLITICAL CONTEXT OF SOCIAL WORK'S FOREBEARS: CHARITY ORGANIZATION SOCIETIES AND SETTLEMENT HOUSE MOVEMENTS

Social work's roots began in the late 1800s. The profession's origins in the settlement houses and charity organization societies are well known. These dual movements created and articulated a dual identity for social work; they provided the frameworks for conceptualizing need, they established the source of blame for the need, they developed the nature and scope of helping, and

THE EVOLUTION OF THE PROFESSION

they set the foundation from which models and roles of social work and the social worker would emerge.

Prior to the first social work course at Columbia University in 1898 (National Association of Social Workers, 2021d), we can examine the two forebears of the profession as "proxies" to gauge, from inception, the profession's complex political ideology. We can examine them to more fully understand how these two movements—both before and accompanying the new profession of "social work"—represented the profession's first forays into the expression of political ideology in the context of helping and social reform. For context, consider how charity organizations and settlement houses were part of a privatized social service delivery system during the Industrial Revolution (DiNitto & Cummins, 2007). Both movements provided assistance to those moving from rural to urban areas, including those who emigrated from other nations; these services included education, childcare, job assistance, citizenship preparation, counseling, and advocacy for social reform (DiNitto & Cummins, 2007). Political machines served as brokers of an organized quid pro quo: "They operated by trading baskets of food, bushes of coal, and favors for the votes of the poor. To finance this early welfare system, the machine offered city contracts, protection, and privileges to business interest, which in return paid off in cash. Aid was provided in a personal fashion without red tape or delays. Recipients did not feel embarrassed or ashamed, for, after all, 'they were trading something valuable—their votes—for the assistance they received'" (DiNitto & Cummins, 2007, p. 39). Absence of any public safety net mechanism, this entwinement with the private sector reflects how both movements needed to

THE EVOLUTION OF THE PROFESSION

fit into conservative notions of political ideology that promoted private versus government-sponsored charity. The question remains to what extent charity organization societies and settlement houses were socialized and perhaps constrained from the further work they may otherwise have wished to initiate.

CHARITY ORGANIZATION SOCIETIES

The charity organization societies (COS) provided assistance to those in greatest need and served to greatly shape the profession's birth. The first COS was founded in 1877 in Buffalo, New York, by Reverend S. Humphreys Gurtee; he used a London model as his template, and in time, COSs gradually multiplied in a number of cities (Hansan, 2013). The societies' specific goals of the were to provide "direct service to individuals and families" and "planning and coordinating efforts" (Dolgoff & Feldstein, 2003, p. 261). In the COS movement, volunteer "friendly visitors" provided companionship, hope, and promotion of hard work to individuals and their families (Hansan, 2013). To address the unemployment, mental illness, and poverty, "the distinctions between public and private relief efforts could be delineated" (Dolgoff & Feldstein, 2003, pp. 261–262).

The COS paradigm initially assumed that the cause of poverty rested within the individual, and this paradigm of helping guided the movement's work. Trattner (1999) writes about the COS's pursuit of addressing poverty by focusing on individual causes. COSs focused on "friendly visiting" in which wealthy individuals would communicate directly with impoverished individuals. Its intent was to end pauperism and resocialize the poor to appreciate the wealthy. Trattner's (1999) observation of this movement illustrates a conservative ideology of not only supporting capitalism but also promoting wealth as intrinsically good and for which all should aspire. Poverty of the era would be eradicated if individuals would just work harder.

What fueled this focus was moral judgment of why someone was impoverished and what could be done to eradicate such poverty. "Leaders" of the "charity organization philosophy . . . believed in the individual-moral concept of poverty" and "accepted the prevailing economic and sociological philosophy that attributed poverty and distress to personal defects and evil acts—sinfulness, failure in the struggle of survival, excessive relief-giving, and so on" (Trattner, 1999, pp. 94–95). To promote teaching based on these conservative values, the Philadelphia Society for Organizing Charitable Relief and Repressing Mendicancy created a *Manual for Visitors Among the Poor* (Dolgoff & Feldstein, 2003). This manual emphasized sympathy and moral encouragement over money, employment over other assistance, the correlation between poverty and disease, and the need for the poor to be educated; in essence, personal responsibility was paramount to eradicate poverty (Dolgoff & Feldstein, 2003, p. 262).

As we can see, the focus on individualistic, deterministic understandings of individual "failings" is well documented. Less known is the more liberating dynamic associated with the charitable organizations as they encouraged a stronger focus on the systemic causes of poverty and inequality. Dolgoff and Feldstein's (2003) observation about the COSs suggests dual, even contradictory, judgments about individuals. In this first insight,

THE EVOLUTION OF THE PROFESSION

the precursor of diversity developed. Dolgoff & Feldstein (2003) observe that the COS movement, from another perspective, was "progressive . . . and planted one of the basic principles of all contemporary social work practice: that each person is different and has to be understood in individual terms (Dolgoff & Feldstein, 2003, p. 263). Additionally, Trattner (1999) describes an additional liberalizing insight from the COS perspective as it matured—that there might be a macro "cause" to each case. "Beginning, then, with a narrow, moralistic, and individualistic attitude toward poverty and its causes, the charity organization movement ultimately fostered the development of a broader point of view. The knowledge of misfortune experienced by hundreds of different families and thousands of individuals eventually induced many representatives of these private agencies to regard the social and economic causes of poverty as more pressing than personal inadequacy—and to realize that only the public could cope with the widespread dependence endemic to modern industrial society" (p. 101).

Situating the COS in Brint's (1994) political ideological framework, we can see that an understanding of poverty, at least at first, reflected more conservative views of political ideology. The opinion that individuals who are poor need to "pull themselves up by their bootstraps" reflects both the Protestant work ethic, and that of individual responsibility, as well as little attention being given to the systemic perspective on the accountability of class. In later years, however, the COS movement did place emphasis on concepts that we would now call self-determinism and diversity—and the role of the "public" to assist in helping with poverty (Trattner, 1999). To this latter point,

THE EVOLUTION OF THE PROFESSION

the very awareness that the public should assist suggests a collective caregiving role for individual moral failing. How the is conceptualized—private charity, local government, or federal government—indicates ideology. More liberal ideology emphasizes the role of the federal government while more moderate and conservative ideologies argue for private charity.

SETTLEMENT HOUSES

In 1886, nine years after the first COS appeared, the first settlement house was founded, and it focused on a different conception of human need and intervention. Trattner (1999) writes that "settlement house residents regarded themselves as social reformers rather than charity workers" (p. 163). Their focus was on social reform and prevention "to bridge the gap between the classes and races, to eliminate the sources of distress, and to improve urban living and working conditions" (p. 163). The first settlement house was called "the Neighborhood Guild," and more than four hundred in total were founded, including Chicago's famous Hull House that was founded in 1899 by Jane Addams and Ellen Gates Starr (National Association of Social Workers, 2021d). The residents of these settlement houses created social welfare organizations to meet emerging neighborhood needs and solve structural problems (Virginia Commonwealth University, 2021).

Their residents and the volunteers, who were precursors to future social workers, "focused on the provision of concrete services, educational and cultural programming and policy advocacy" (Reisch, 2022). Their history is a telling response to the COS's history as it reflected more of a focus on prevention (Trattner, 1999). Trattner (1999) shares Jane Addams's critique of COS staff who "were cold and unemotional, too impersonal and stingy, that they were pervaded by a negative pseudoscientific spirit"; she argued, "Their vocabulary . . . was one of 'don't give,' 'don't act,' 'don't do this or that'; all they gave the poor was advice—and for that they probably sent the Almighty a bill" (Trattner, 1999, p. 97).

While settlement houses were broadly considered progressive compared to COSs, the reality was that their work—and ultimately the inherent political ideology guiding their initiatives—was influenced by their funding mechanism. Trattner (1999) references a study that found a correlation between settlement houses' programs to address social and economic problems and the degree they received support from business-funded community chests. The study author writes, "the 'more dependent a settlement house was on a community chest, the more conservative it was on social issues,' whatever they happened to be" (Trattner, 1999, p. 264). Thus, in the 1920s and 1930s, settlement houses that were more independent of business funding functioned more as true community-organizing entities, whereas settlement houses dependent on business funding were seen as having lost their "reformist zeal" (p. 264).

As we reflect on the political ideology of settlement houses, we see how the funding stream determined how "liberal" the settlement house could act. This is particularly relevant in the assumed history of the liberal to progressive ideology of settlement houses. They firmly stood to the left of the COS, at least in concept, by examining structural factors for oppression

THE EVOLUTION OF THE PROFESSION

and methods of rectifying inequities. Yet, because they varied in their reliance on these community chests, each individual settlement house's ideology was dependent on the level of monied interests that funded their efforts. Therefore, perhaps we can look at the social movement of settlement houses as a liberal response to the conservative COS, and yet, organizationally, the degree to which their work reflected liberal ideology—or a more moderate or conservative ideology—was promoted or constrained by their funding stream.

Looking further, this expansive reflection that challenges settlement houses' well-known, "monolithic" liberal political ideology extends to the inherent middle-class and white values associated with the movement (Trattner, 1999). True, the settlement house movement focused on economic and social change (Trattner, 1999). However, both it and the COS movements reflected middle-class values and "both were more interested in order and efficiency than in justice and equality, and each, in its own way, helped to rationalize and stabilize the social and economic order of the day" (Trattner, 1999, pp. 167–169).

With these insights, we can see the complexity of the political ideology reflected in the settlement house movement that was dictated beyond the funding stream. Using our political ideological lens for assessment, they appeared to be both more liberal in their approach to macro reform and yet this "reform" was based in a conservative socialization to dominant paradigms of power that privileged individuals who were white and middle-class. The settlement house movement did not challenge capitalism. However, while regulating the poor in a given capitalist system is conservative, enacting laws that support

THE EVOLUTION OF THE PROFESSION

individuals' rights and recourse when those rights are violated does reflect a more liberal perspective. Therefore, Trattner's (1999) assessment provides evidence of the range of political ideology inherent within the settlement house movement and challenges traditional notions of their ideology.

CHARITY ORGANIZATION SOCIETIES AND SETTLEMENT HOUSES IN POLITICAL CONTEXT

We briefly reviewed the purposes and critiques of charity organization societies and settlement houses. These movements both sought to ameliorate social problems with sometimes conflicting assumptions of why problems occur and underlying values of how these problems should be solved. While both are lauded in social work lore as the professions' forebears, COSs have been perceived stereotypically as more conservative than the more liberal settlement houses. While this is largely true (Trattner, 1999), evidence suggests that COSs promoted more liberal concepts of government intervention for individual problems, and settlement houses helped socialize individuals into middle-class values, and at times, relied on funding streams that steered them into moderate and conservative work. An examination of the concurrent conservatizing and liberalizing forces associated with these two movements is found in table 2.1.

As we reflect on the emergence of these two tracks of social work, we can now more deeply understand the political context associated with each. Constructs of political ideology (Baradat & Phillips, 2020; Brint, 1994; Knight, 1999) help provide the context of views on social change, the regulation of the poor,

THE EVOLUTION OF THE PROFESSION

TABLE 2.1 Political Ideologies and Social Work Forebears: Charity Organization Societies and Settlement Houses

	Charity Organization Societies	Settlement Houses
Conservatizing Forces	• Explicit purpose of advice giving	• Regulation of the poor
	• Moral judgment	• Grounded in middle-class values
	• Status quo maintaining	• Some funded by corporate community chests
	• Regulation of the poor	
Liberalizing Forces	• In time, examined structural factors of poverty	• Explicit purpose to enact social reform
	• Forebear for self-determination	• Much of work devoted to community organizing and promoting civil rights
	• Forebear for diversity	• Some funded independent of corporate community chests

Source: Draws on Dolgoff & Feldstein (2003); Trattner (1999).

the role of government in assistance, and the underlying values of the human condition. While Brint's (1994) conception is culturally located in a much later era, it is still useful in linking these two groundbreaking movements of the profession with political ideology. These dynamics show that even with

■ 44 ■

THE EVOLUTION OF THE PROFESSION

the historic backdrop of the profession, political ideology was neither simplistic nor monolithic.

BIRTH OF PROFESSION—CONTINUATION OF TWO POLITICAL IDEOLOGICAL MOVEMENTS

These two movements "dramatically influenced" the birth of the profession and "their confluence within the major stream of social work" (Dolgoff & Feldstein, 2003, p. 265). As already discussed, social work emerged as a profession beginning in 1898 when the first training course for charity workers was provided in New York; by 1919, there were fifteen training schools devoted to advancing social work training (Trattner, 1999). Due to the need to manage contracts for relief funds, COSs hired staff, and with the combination of training programs, the professionalization of social work began (Trattner, 1999).

While professional charity relief training began, the settlement houses continued to thrive. We can see an example of political ideology—the degree of support for militarism and war—in the World War I activism of members of the two movements. Trattner (1999) observes settlement house members and social reformers advocated against World War I while the majority of caseworkers with the COS movement supported going to war. This distinction was seen no less by the "mothers" of both movements: "While Jane Addams and many of her colleagues were actively involved in the peace movement, Mary Richmond and many of her colleagues were actively involved in the Home Service Division of the American Red

· 45 ·

THE EVOLUTION OF THE PROFESSION

Cross. And revealingly, although Jane Addams would receive a number of honorary degrees during her lifetime, not one came from a school of social work; in 1921 Smith College conferred such an honor on Mary Richmond" (pp. 259–260).

Here, we can see that individual social workers' political ideologies may be a determinant in their field of practice—as evidenced by association with these two movements. Reflected in current standards, keep in mind that Brint's (1994) antimilitarism reflects a New Left ideology while subscription to war indicates ideology somewhere within the liberal to New Right spectrum.

As the war concluded, the two movements continued down markedly different paths. Trained caseworkers replaced voluntary friendly visitors while settlement house residents' gravitas was declining (Trattner, 1999). We can see evidence of this dual focus even more as we review the emergence of interweaving professionalization and treatment on the one hand and continued social reform on the other. In response to Flexner's 1915 infamous chastisement that social work was not a profession, social work embraced its professionalization through the lens of psychological treatment and the influence of Freud in the 1920s (Trattner, 1999). Trattner (1999) describes how some social workers aligned and "identified themselves with the psychiatric clinical team rather than with social reformers or even social caseworkers, who seemed old fashioned if not passe" (p. 261). This shift in focus "from 'cause' to 'function,' to use Porter Lee's terms" resulted in social workers moving "from advocating reform to efficiently rendering technical services" (Trattner, p. 1999, p. 267). This shift

■ 46 ■

THE EVOLUTION OF THE PROFESSION

also resulted in similar views of poverty cloaked in new language. "The unworthy poor had become the emotionally disturbed or deprived poor" (Trattner, 1999, p. 262).

In the early years of the profession, a shift occurred as a result of professionalization. In 1930, social work was listed as a profession per the U. S. Census (Trattner, 1999). In its quest to attain professional status and all of the concomitant work that is required, much of the profession became enveloped in conservative ideology and reduced one of its two emphases—the liberal ideology of social reform—to ally with Freud and develop psychiatric casework and enjoy the benefits of professionalization. Even the social reform focus of the profession, while still present, declined with this competing professional interest (Trattner, 1999). We can see then that within a few decades of its birth, by today's standards, social work became increasingly enveloped in conservative ideology.

Specht and Courtney (1994) describe this trend by referencing the "angels" who cared about professionalization and provided admirable assistance to those in need and yet had "abandoned" their mission to social work roots. They were describing the odd trajectory that social work took in which it sought professionalization at the expense of the "true" social justice roots of the settlement house movement. Over time, much of the energy and focus that social workers devoted to community organizing for the welfare of women and children, seniors, those with disabilities, the poor, and immigrants shifted toward the professionalization movement and the conservatizing nature of this quest.

THE EVOLUTION OF THE PROFESSION

THE NEW DEAL AND THE PROFESSION'S POLITICAL IDEOLOGY

As part of the profession's focus on function and treatment, by extension, a more conservative promotion of the status quo flourished. Yet, in this era, the social reform branch of the profession that was moving full-speed ahead reflected a liberal ideology. This was seen centrally in the role of the profession vis à vis President Roosevelt's New Deal response to the Great Depression. The stark and sudden impact of the Depression provided fertile ground for Americans to reconsider economic reform (DiNitto & Cummins, 2007). "The [D]epression also prompted a resurgence of interest among many social workers in social reform as well as old-fashioned relief. What good was psychiatric treatment when millions of citizens were unemployed and whole families were starving?" (p. 297)

For a nation that had been so decimated by the Great Depression, the Roosevelt administration sought to formally create a permanent safety net for some of the country's most vulnerable citizens. The New Deal sought sweeping changes to revolutionize social welfare—in benefit, coverage, and delivery—with an awesome commitment by the federal government. The new focus on public welfare was in stark contrast to the "'rugged individualism' so popular in the earlier days of the country. . . . The objectives of the New Deal were "relief, recovery, and reform" (DiNitto & Cummins, 2007, p. 40).

The program's components were comprehensive and tried to predict a range of problems that could be prevented. The creation of landmark legislation such as the Social Security Act,

• 48 •

THE EVOLUTION OF THE PROFESSION

the Works Progress Administration, the Civilian Conservation Corps, and the Fair Labor Standards Act provided public assistance, jobs, and minimum wage to numerous Americans (DiNitto & Cummins, 2007). The New Deal contributed to an expanded sense of federalism with increased federal responsibility and oversight over social welfare. "Although it preserved a major role of the states in the operation of some of its provisions, it established for all time that the U. S. government could have a direct, helping relationship with its citizens" (Ginsberg, 1998, p. 26).

The role of social workers in these social welfare efforts cannot be understated. We see a continued clear focus on liberal ideologies as articulated by Brint (1994) on underlying values and the role of the welfare state in human betterment. The publication of *The Response of Social Work to the Depression* showed the profession's support for organized labor (Trattner, 1999). As part of Roosevelt's administration and his New Deal social policy approach, social workers took part in creating this liberal movement of social welfare that impacted the entire nation. The profession of social worker gained increased legitimacy and might as social workers played a key role in increasing the safety net for Americans (Trattner,1999)

We can examine the particular contributions of social workers in these efforts (Trattner, 1999). For example, Frances Perkins was appointed secretary of labor by Roosevelt and led efforts to create the Social Security Act. Harry Hopkins was appointed head of the Federal Emergency Relief Act and oversaw job creation and income assistance for the unemployed during the Depression. Martha Eliot and Katharine Lenroot provided

■ 49 ■

leadership to the U.S. Children's Bureau. These and other social work leaders catapulted the profession to an "unprecedented prestige in American life as a result of the [Great D]epression and the New Deal" (Trattner, 1999, p. 298). Interestingly, Frank Bruno, a social work professor, argued the Social Security Act was too moderate and should have been more sweeping in its reform efforts (Trattner, 1999).

And yet, during this era, the profession significantly focused its identity formation on allegiance to Freud and his psychological treatment, all while continuing to wrestle with its identity (Trattner, 1999). This reflects a bifurcated response with a significant component of the profession undergirded by liberal ideology relating to the role of the federal government in social welfare and the individual treatment section focused more on professionalization than macro change. To the latter, this focus on professionalization and the status quo suggests, sociologically, a withdrawal of progressive activism and a subsequent connection to moderate to conservative ideology's reliance on the status quo.

SOCIAL WELFARE AND SOCIAL WORK IN THE 1960s

The 1960s are well known for civil unrest, civil rights, and the further transformation of the social welfare system. As the decade began, the reality of almost forty million people, including African American and Hispanic individuals living

THE EVOLUTION OF THE PROFESSION

in poverty, became front and center; "civil rights and the depressed economic condition of these individuals became the issues of the days" (DiNitto & Cummins, 2007, p. 41). Under the Kennedy administration, the food stamp pilot program began and the Community Mental Health Act was signed (DiNitto & Cummins 2007). The Johnson administration's War on Poverty and Great Society were realized with the passage of the Economic Opportunity Act of 1964 and the advent of the Medicare, Medicaid, and Food Stamps programs, as well as Head Start preschool, community action agencies, and model cities program (DiNitto & Cummins, 2007). The Great Society's programs served millions of American even though some debate the success of War on Poverty (Trattner, 1999).

This era's focus on civil rights was sparked by the successes of *Brown v. Board of Education*, Rosa Parks, and Martin Luther King's Montgomery, Alabama, bus boycott. The Civil Rights Act, which addressed African American suffrage and equal access in employment, education, and public accommodation, was passed (Ginsberg, 1998). The Voting Rights Act provided for the inspection of elections to ensure racial nondiscrimination. However, the Equal Rights Amendment, guaranteeing gender civil rights, did not get enough momentum to become law.

The National Association of Social Workers (NASW) formed in 1955 from the merger of a number of social work associations (Trattner, 1999). This strength poised NASW to take on a leadership role for social work and its causes. This position was in light of the fact that "social workers and their services had fallen from grace" because the Social Security Act

THE EVOLUTION OF THE PROFESSION

amendments began to favor concrete services over casework services (Trattner, 1999, p. 329).

In this era, social work became less apathetic and conservative with respect to maintaining the status quo. "The social work profession itself finally responded to the changed political climate. In the early 1960s, sparked by the War on Poverty, community organization returned to its settlement house roots. It redirected its focus from coordinating services to mobilizing clients for community self-determination and the redistribution of resources" (Abramovitz, 1998, p. 516).

This redirection from service coordination to client mobilization was palpable in the profession (Abramovitz, 1998). Younger social workers identified more as "advocates" than "therapists" (Trattner, 1999, p. 345). Macro practice increasingly became a focus for social work education, "placing more emphasis on such things as group work and community organizing, public administration, and social policy, and even opening up new field placements in militant community groups" (Trattner, 1999, p. 345). The Council on Social Work Education (CSWE) pushed for these schools to influence social policy (Trattner, 1999). NASW hired a lobbyist and revised its bylaws to promote social action "to prevent and alleviate 'deprivation, distress, and strain' (Trattner, 1999, p. 345). This rallying call was even heard from Helen Harris Perlman, who was known for championing casework (Trattner, 1999). This liberal to New Left view on structural change and increased public welfare exemplified the political ideology of much of the profession in this era.

■ 52 ■

THE EVOLUTION OF THE PROFESSION

SOCIAL WORK POLITICAL IDEOLOGY IN THE 1970S AND THE REAGAN/BUSH ERA

President Nixon's administration, "determined to clean up the 'welfare mess,' proposed another type of reform in the early 1970s—a guaranteed annual income for all poor people" (DiNitto & Cummins, 2007). Under Nixon, the Supplemental Security Income (SSI) social welfare program was initiated to help individuals with disabilities, or seniors, on a limited income (DiNitto & Cummins, 2007). The Occupational Safety and Health Act (OSHA) and the Child Abuse Prevention and Treatment Act (CAPTA) were also passed (Ginsberg, 1998). Nixon proposed a guaranteed income and Family Assistance Plan to provide cash assistance to people who are aged, blind, or disabled and living in poverty, but these proposals did not pass Congress (DiNitto & Cummins, 2007).[1] However, he vetoed the Comprehensive Child Care Act (Ginsberg, 1998). We can see that while Nixon did support some "liberal" social welfare programs, he "continued to lambaste the Great Society, 'big spenders,' and liberals, especially federal civil servants, who he said were undermining conservative programs, and social workers, who in his opinion, coddled the poor" (Trattner, 1999, p. 349). Following Nixon, President Ford was not a friend to social welfare, and President Carter initiated the Cabinet-level Departments of Education and Energy, and a revamped Health and Human Services (Trattner, 1999).

When President Ronald Reagan was elected in 1980, the Reagan Revolution began. His administration's focus on free

• 53 •

THE EVOLUTION OF THE PROFESSION

enterprise, the doctrine of "peace through [military] strength," a balanced budget, tax cuts largely for the wealthy, and suspicion of welfare recipients culminated in "Reaganomics" or "supply-side economics" (Trattner, 1999). Under Reagan's watch, major social welfare programs including food stamps, housing vouchers, income assistance, child care, and school lunches had their budgets reduced, in the billions of dollars, as the thought was such voluminous programs fostered economic dependency and the continued maintenance of a large welfare state. This philosophy saw a shift to states administering social welfare programs as "block grants" in the New Federalism paradigm (Trattner, 1999).

These initiatives, reflecting the rise of cultural and fiscal conservatism, had major consequences on many Americans (Reisch, 2022). Poverty rates soared "particularly among children (to nearly 25 percent), young families, and persons of color" (Reisch, 2022, p. 84). People with HIV/AIDS were long neglected by the federal government until the passage of the Ryan White Act (Reisch, 2022). Issues of homelessness and immigration/refugees were neglected (Reisch, 2022). The devolution of federal services to state and local control was in full swing (Ginsberg,1998).

Eventually, the Ryan White Act was passed to provide needed funding and services to individuals with HIV/AIDS. Attempts to help people struggling financially from the recession included a nearly $10 billion aid package and the Family Support Act (Reisch, 2022). The Earned Income Tax Credit (EITC) was refunded. President Bush continued Reagan's conservative efforts. Additionally, Bush passed the Americans with

THE EVOLUTION OF THE PROFESSION

Disabilities Act of 1990 and led the United States to war in the Middle East.

In these two decades, the social work profession began to express activism toward liberal and even New Left political ideology with efforts from both NASW and CSWE (Abramovitz, 1998). "In the early 1970s NASW rejected the longstanding separation of professional and political activities. It created Political Action for Candidate Endorsement and Education and Legislative Action Network to support liberal policies and politicians" (Abramovitz, 1998, p. 517). CSWE mandated curricular changes to focus more on politics, diversity, and social policy (Abramovitz, 1998). Members of both organizations engaged more with peace, justice, and human rights movements internationally (Abramovitz, 1998).

Social workers in the 1970s were frustrated with the profession's focus on professionalization over reform-mindedness and apathy; consequently, these frustrations led to the birth of social work organizations such as the Association of Black Social Workers, Association of Women and Social Work (and their journal *Affilia*), and Radical Alliance of Social Service Workers (and their journal *Catalyst*, which became known as the *Journal of Progressive Human Services*) (Abramovitz, 1998). In the 1980s, the social work association known as the Bertha Capen Reynolds Society focused on progressive issues such as promoting civil rights and trade unions (Abramovitz, 1998). Yet the journey toward professionalization continued and was espoused by both micro-oriented schools in the profession—the diagnostic and the functional; as of the early 1980s, social work licensure extended to twenty-nine states (Dolgoff & Feldstein, 2003).

THE EVOLUTION OF THE PROFESSION

Therefore, while some liberal and progressive organizations and journals emerged, these political eras had many social workers prioritizing professionalization and licensure.

THE CLINTON ERA AND SOCIAL WORK POLITICAL IDEOLOGY

President Clinton's administration supported initiatives that reflected both the conservative and liberal brands of the Democratic Party; Clinton's presidency is characterized as "neo-liberalism" (Reisch, 2022). One of the chief hallmarks of his presidency was the passage of the Personal Responsibility and Work Opportunity Act (PRWORA) of 1996; in effect, this law overhauled the delivery of income assistance for the poor. It replaced Aid to Families with Dependent Children (AFDC) with Temporary Aid to Needy Families (TANF) and established work requirements and lifetime limits to receive such welfare; these distributions were in the form of block grants to nonpublic organizations, including faith-based organizations (Reisch, 2022; Trattner, 1999). Additionally, income assistance programs such as SSI and food stamps were withheld from immigrants (Trattner, 1999). Clinton also signed the Defense of Marriage Act, which reaffirmed marriage could only be accessed by heterosexual couples.

However, liberal ideologies were also represented by the Clinton administration; he signed the Family and Medical Leave Act, extended unemployment compensation, sought free vaccinations for all American children, and allowed Planned

THE EVOLUTION OF THE PROFESSION

Parenthood and other clinics to receive federal funding (Trattner, 1999). Furthermore, he championed a health-care overhaul to provide access to all Americans as well as increased the EITC and established the State Children's Health Insurance Program (SCHIP) (Reisch, 2022).

Similar to the 1970s and 1980s, the 1990s represented politically diverse professional engagement for social work as it continued its trajectory from "charity to enterprise" (Abramovitz, 1998). Abramovitz (1998) remarks that "social workers, along with many others in the liberal community, remained strangely silent while a punitive welfare reform bill worked its way through Congress and the state legislatures" (p. 521). This apathy reflected a growing conservative ideology associated with the status quo; again, while not avowedly conservative in terms of policy promotion, this focus on enterprise building over social action may reflect such a conservative ideology. Yet, some liberal to progressive ideology was observed by the profession as "the activist wing of social work" confronted social workers' apolitical views of the profession and "ensured that the profession remained an arena of political struggle" (Abramovitz, 1998, p. 521).

THE TWENTY-FIRST CENTURY: POLITICS AND THE PROFESSION

The compassionate conservatism reflected in the George W. Bush administration reflected an increased focus on homeland security post 9/11 and increased privatization (Reisch, 2022).

THE EVOLUTION OF THE PROFESSION

Under Bush, PRWORA was reauthorized with even more strict work requirements and the No Child Left Behind Act was created to enact education reform (Reisch, 2022). Yet Bush showcased a more liberal ideology with the passage of Medicare Part D for prescription drug benefits, increased funding for SCHIP, and increased funding for HIV/AIDS throughout the globe (Reisch, 2022).

The Obama administration then supported the $300 billion American Reinvestment and Recovery Act (ARRA), which addressed the recession and bailed out the American automobile industry (Reisch, 2022). Race to the Top replaced No Child Left Behind, food assistance increased, and additional funding was provided for job training, childcare, and violence prevention (Reisch, 2022). President Obama signed the Deferred Action for Childhood Arrivals (DACA) resolution, which "protected the children of undocumented immigrants brought to the United States from deportation" (Reisch, 2022, p. 91). His most famous victory was his passage of the Patient Protection and Affordable Care Act (ACA), a sweeping attempt to reform the nation's health-care system (Reisch, 2022). During his administration, the Supreme Court upheld ACA but banned the requirement for Medicaid expansion to all states (Reisch, 2022).

The Trump administration has "reflected an unusual combination of right-wing neo-populism, supply-side economics, the cultural values of the president's evangelical supporters, and traditional conservative antisocial welfare attitudes" (Reisch, 2022, p. 29). Under Trump, anti-immigrant and anti-Muslim rhetoric was matched with an attempt to bar immigrants from

■ 58 ■

mostly Muslim nations (Reisch, 2022) and a rhetorical attack on four U.S. Congresswomen, including two who were Muslim, to go back to their own countries. This reaction to immigration continued with a revisiting of asylum policy for undocumented immigrants, the legal limbo of DACA recipients, the push for border security as a response to an immigrant crisis on the southern border, and the separation of children from parents in undocumented families. Aside from immigration, civil rights on federal protections for women and abortion, and transgender individuals in the military, continued with his initial policies (Reisch, 2022). Conservative ideology continued to be reflected in the Tax Cuts and Jobs Act, which gave permanent tax cuts to corporations and temporary tax cuts to citizens and requires states to purge voter lists that may be discriminatory (Berman, 2017). Additionally, the Supreme Court ruled, in two separate cases, in favor of business owners' religious freedom to deny a service to a same-sex couple and to not provide birth control to its employees.

More recently, the Biden administration was successful in passing bipartisan legislation that provided trillions in relief and recovery related to the COVID-19 pandemic, including the Coronavirus Aid, Relief, and Economic Security Act (CARES) and the American Rescue Plan Act (ARPA). Biden also passed bipartisan infrastructure legislation but found his safety net of the Build Back Better legislation and improved voting rights legislation stalled (Peter G. Peterson Foundation, 2021). A scaled-down version of Build Back Better that focused on climate change and prescription drug price control was realized in the Inflation Reduction Act.

THE EVOLUTION OF THE PROFESSION

The social work response in this era reflected similar stances as the recent prior eras. NASW championed the Obama and Biden administrations and showed great concern for Trump's election, as well as the insurrection on January 6, 2021 (National Association of Social Workers, 2015; 2016; 2021c; 2021e). The policy statements in response to these three administrations reflected liberal ideology. Further, NASW continued to champion the federal Social Work Reinvestment Act, which sought federal funding of the profession; while regularly introduced by social workers in the U.S. Congress for the past thirteen years, it is still awaiting passage (Clark, 2008; National Association of Social Workers, 2019). Also pertaining to Congress, the Congressional Social Work Caucus was created in 2010 to champion social work-related causes. Therefore, we see a consistent liberal ideology reflected through NASW's responses to the Obama, Trump, and Biden administrations as well as proposed policy through Congressional initiatives. Yet how much the rank and file are involved in these efforts—with, sadly, a declining NASW membership of some thirty thousand members over the past decade—is less known. This trend is coupled with a profession that seeks continued professionalization with winnowing activism and as a result, support for the status quo. The contradiction endures.

Chapter Three

RESEARCH ON POLITICAL DIVERSITY AND SOCIAL WORK

THE SCOPE of research in the field of social work and political diversity remains wide open. This chapter examines the research literature both historically and with more recent inquiry. Literature before Rosenwald (2006a; 2006b) and Rosenwald and Hyde's (2006) research on political diversity of social workers included findings from empirical studies that discuss, in some form, the political ideologies of social workers. As Rosenwald's research was the first comprehensive study on political ideology and its impact on professional affiliation and practice, scholarship before this study is presented first.[1]

HISTORICAL RESEARCH

Drawing on the conceptions of political ideology, the following studies examined aspects of political ideology. Significant

RESEARCH ON POLITICAL DIVERSITY AND SOCIAL WORK

findings are shared by theme, with the theme typically represented by a demographic or professional variable. In some studies, political ideology was but one correlate in a larger research question (e.g., Epstein, 1969; Reeser and Epstein, 1990). In other studies, political ideology served as the dependent variable itself (e.g., Abbott, 1988; Wagner, 1990). The studies included social workers and social work students alone (e.g., Abbott, 1999, Fisher, Weedman, Alex & Stout, 2001, Wagner, 1990) as well as including them in comparison to members of other professions (Abbott, 1988; Hendershot & Grimm, 1974; Henry, Sims & Spray, 1971; Rubinstein, 1994). Finally, the literature is divided into those studies that examined social workers in practice (e.g., Csikai, 1999; Lev-Wiesel & Friedlander, 1999; Reeser & Epstein, 1990; Rubinstein, 1994; Sagi & Dvir, 1993) and those in education (e.g., Fisher et al., 2001; Varley, 1968; Sheridan, Wilmer & Atcheson, 1994).

In the early literature, as an independent variable, political ideology was operationalized as "political philosophy," "political party affiliation," and sometimes as both. Overall, social workers tend to be liberal and Democrats. For example, Reeser and Epstein (1990) and Epstein (1969) examined political party affiliation as a correlate of political activism. Similarities were found despite their studies being done seventeen years apart. Specifically, in 1968, 73 percent were Democrat, 9 percent were Republican, 11 percent had no party identification, and 7 percent were New Left; in 1990, 77 percent of social workers sampled stated they were Democrat, 9 percent were Republican, 10 percent had no party identification, and 4 percent were New Left.

RESEARCH ON POLITICAL DIVERSITY AND SOCIAL WORK

When considering only social workers, Abbott (1988) found that an individual's political ideology explained the most variance on her Professional Opinion Scale. Like Epstein (1969) and Reeser and Epstein's (1990) studies, the percentage of Democrats was similar to Abbott's (1988) findings—approximately two-thirds of the sample. Abbott (1988) linked Republican Party membership with conservative political philosophy and Democrat Party membership with liberal political philosophy. However, in a later study, Abbott (1999) stated political philosophy is problematic because her sample of international social workers had different cultural meanings of liberal and conservative.

Examining political philosophy instead of political party affiliation, Varley (1968), Henry et al. (1971), and Hodge's (2003) research suggests social workers are less liberal than may be commonly thought. In a study of social work students, Varley (1968) found that 55.3 percent were moderates, 32.9 percent were liberals, and 11.8 percent were conservatives. In Henry et al.'s (1971) study that included psychiatric social workers among other mental health professionals, 42.9 percent said "strong liberal," 50.8 percent said "moderate liberal," and 6.3 percent said "conservative." With the introduction of a "moderate" category, Hodge (2003), using General Social Survey data, found that 46 percent of social workers with graduate degrees self-reported as liberal, 40 percent as moderate, and 14 percent as conservative. Additionally, 36 percent of social workers with a bachelor of social work (BSW) were liberal, 39 percent were moderate, and 26 percent were conservative (Hodge, 2003). As contrasted with Epstein (1969) and Reeser and Epstein's (1990) studies,

· 63 ·

RESEARCH ON POLITICAL DIVERSITY AND SOCIAL WORK

these differences may be due to the difference in measuring political ideology as political philosophy versus political party affiliation.

These liberal and conservative political ideologies may also relate to activism. *Traditional activism* seeks social change outside of social institutions and is more rapid and wide reaching. *Institutional activism* takes place within the structure of social welfare agencies, for example, and promotes a more incremental view of change. Epstein (1969) and Reeser and Epstein (1990) found conservative social workers involved with more institutional activism in the 1980s while liberal social workers were affiliated with more traditional activism in the 1960s.

Little focus appears to be given in the literature to studies involving New Left social workers (and no literature was found on studies of New Right social workers). Two studies serve as examples of research on New Left social workers (Wagner, 1990; Fisher et al., 2001) with somewhat different findings. Wagner (1990) examined radical social workers, their commitment to ideology, and their experience with professionalization. He found that most were influenced by the 1960s movements and continued to maintain their radical ideology despite waning political activism. Additionally, Wagner (1990) learned that the conservative nature of the social work profession seems incompatible with activism.

Fisher et al.'s (2001) study of alumni and students associated with a New Left graduate social work program examined these ideologies as well. In their findings, 76 percent of graduates identified with the "social justice" label the most, 66 percent with the "feminist" label ; and 10 percent with the "Marxist/socialist

• 64 •

RESEARCH ON POLITICAL DIVERSITY AND SOCIAL WORK

and/or radical" labels. Similar to Wagner's (1990) research, Fisher et al. (2001) found that alumni maintained their ideologies. However, unlike Wagner's (1990) research, strong professional identity and progressive (New Left) practice were maintained after graduation. Discussing the difference, Fisher et al. (2001) reported their findings may have been more similar to Wagner's (1990) findings if the participants in Fisher et al.'s (2001) study had their "radical" practice clarified.

Though all of these studies focused on political ideology of individual social workers, one study examined a related area at the mezzo level. Epstein (1988) examined the relationship between political ideology, social welfare agencies, and their leadership in the voluntary sector. The agencies' perspectives on social policies conformed to the conservative political ideology of the Reagan administration. Although the agencies' boards of directors were conservative, their directors tended to be slightly more liberal. Specifically, 62 percent of directors of social welfare agencies were at least moderately conservative, which signified more liberalness than their boards of directors. Epstein (1988) explained, "In contrast to their boards' attitudes, the directors described themselves as somewhat more liberal with slightly more expansive views toward taxation and the provision of welfare, and much more positive pro-choice views toward abortion. Moreover, far fewer directors characterized their own general political orientation as 'conservative' or 'moderately conservative'" (p. 107).

Political ideology of social workers was also studied in relation to other professions and the general public. Social workers tended to be more liberal than their professional counterparts.

BSW social work students held more liberal beliefs in basic rights and social responsibility than undergraduates in business, social science, nursing, and education (Abbott, 1988). These social work students also had more liberal scores on believing in individual freedom than those other students (Abbott, 1988). MSW students had more liberal scores on equal rights than medical students, as well as more liberal scores on social responsibility and individual freedom than business graduate students (Abbott, 1988).

The majority of the time, social work students self-identified as more liberal than other groups of undergraduate or graduate students surveyed even when the studies controlled for "family income and gender at the undergraduate level, and race and gender at the graduate level" (Abbott, 1988, p. 57). Abbott (1988) remarked that important covariates at the undergraduate and graduate levels included, respectively, race and current residence, and family income and religion.

Earlier research explored the political ideologies of social workers, health professionals, and teachers. For example, in examining health-care professionals' support for legitimate reasons to have abortions, Werley et al. (1973) found that at least 82 percent of social workers supported at least one reason for abortion, which was the highest percentage compared to physicians and nurses. Social workers were more liberal than nurses, perhaps because social workers deal with the larger psychosocial context of the client compared to the narrower health focus of nurses (Hendershot & Grimm, 1974). When social workers were compared to teachers, they scored higher than teachers on

RESEARCH ON POLITICAL DIVERSITY AND SOCIAL WORK

value dimensions that reflected, in part, a more liberal political ideology (McLeod & Meyer, 1967).

Similar findings are usually found in comparing social workers to other mental health professionals. Henry et al. (1971) did not find a significant difference between social workers and psychotherapists. However, in exploring values and mental health professionals, Jensen and Bergin (1988) learned 70 percent of social workers self-reported their values as liberal compared to 50 percent of psychologists, 44 percent of marriage and family therapists, and 33 percent of psychiatrists. This finding is similar to Rubinstein's (1994) findings that suggested Israeli social workers and social work students were more liberal than psychiatrists.

Finally, social workers are more liberal than the general public. Social workers tended to hold this ideology in 1975 and 1979–1980, the two different time periods that Koeske and Crouse (1981) measured political ideology. Hodge (2003) also supports this finding. Exploring differences in values between social workers, the working class, and other middle-class workers, Hodge (2003) used questions on political issues (e.g., death penalty, abortion, and welfare) from the General Social Survey to gauge political ideology. He found that regardless of degree, social workers have a more liberal political ideology, both economically and socially, than non-social workers.

In sum, social workers generally espoused a liberal political ideology rather than a conservative ideology. This ideology holds consistent whether the studies are of social workers— alone or comparative in nature.

DEMOGRAPHIC CORRELATES OF POLITICAL IDEOLOGY

The demographic correlates of political ideology (age, gender, race/ethnicity, sexual orientation, class, and religion/spirituality) were discussed to varying degrees in the literature. Because the literature on political ideology of social workers is quite small and findings were sometimes inconsistent, it was premature to state that any particular finding suggests a definitive correlate of political ideologies of social workers. The literature on age, gender, race/ethnicity, and sexual orientation appears sparse and inconsistent and is presented first. The information on class and religion/spirituality is more conclusive and is presented next.

The effect of age on political ideology was inconclusive. Age was not a significant correlate of political ideology in McLeod and Meyer's (1967) study. Yet older age was associated with more liberal political ideologies (Abbott, 1988; 1999) though the 1999 study examined international social workers.

With respect to gender, female social workers are more liberal than male social workers in terms of social work values (Hayes & Varley, 1965; Kidneigh & Lundberg, 1958). However, men were identified as being more liberal in Abbott's (1999) study of international social workers.

Race emerged as a significant predictor of political ideology (Abbott, 1999; McLeod & Meyer, 1967). In Abbott's (1999) international study, Caucasian social workers were more liberal (with an intervening correlation of higher income) than non-Caucasian social workers. With respect to nationality, social workers from Asian countries tended to be more

RESEARCH ON POLITICAL DIVERSITY AND SOCIAL WORK

conservative than social workers from North America, Europe, Australia, and New Zealand (Abbott, 1999).

With respect to sexual orientation, a larger proportion of gay, lesbian, and bisexual alumni and students were affiliated with the political social work concentration than in the general social work school (Fisher et al., 2001). Though Fisher et al. (2001) did not comment on this group with particular findings, their affiliation suggests that New Left social work may be of particular interest to gay, lesbian, and bisexual alumni and students. The research did not examine students or alumni who were transgender.

Regarding class, Varley (1963) found a correlation between socioeconomic status and value change. In particular, the wealthier the social work student, the more likely they were to favor helping the poor with more government intervention (Grimm & Orten, 1973). Additionally, higher incomes associated with more liberalness (Abbott, 1999).

The literature suggests that social workers with less religious or spiritual beliefs were more liberal. For example, fewer religious social workers tended to be more liberal on issues relating to euthanasia and assisted suicide. In McLeod and Meyer's (1967) study, social workers who did not report having an identified religion scored higher on those social work values associated with more liberal political ideology. When compared to other mental health professionals, social workers agreed with values relating to religion the least (Jensen & Bergin, 1988). This skepticism of religious values was partially found in Sheridan, Wilmer, and Atcheson's (1994) study of social work faculty's views on including religious and spiritual content in the curriculum. They found that a majority of faculty favored a course's inclusion in the curriculum, yet only 20.8 percent would require it compared to 62.4 percent who would support its inclusion as an elective.

With respect to particular demonstrations, McLeod and Meyer's (1967) study, Jewish and nonreligious social workers were more liberal than Christian social workers. However, in Abbott's (1999) international study, Jewish, Catholic, and Protestant social workers were more liberal than other religious groups (that Abbott did not identify).

PROFESSIONAL CORRELATES OF POLITICAL IDEOLOGY

Five professional correlates were related to political ideology: degree, employment status, type of work setting, years of work experience, and type of social work function. Higher educational degrees appear to contribute to liberal political ideology. With regard to the related variable of education itself, there was some evidence that it also increased liberal political ideology. For example, Varley (1968) found some increase in liberal ideology, as measured by valuing equal rights, from admission to graduation for social work students. Social workers with master's degrees in social work were more liberal than social workers with bachelor's degrees in social work (Abbott, 1988; Csikai, 1999, Hodge, 2003).

Regarding employment status, Brint (1994) drew on his research that employment is often the decisive influence on the political views of professionals, including social workers.

• 70 •

RESEARCH ON POLITICAL DIVERSITY AND SOCIAL WORK

Once the individual is employed, professional characteristics play a role in the formation of their political ideology. Type of work setting (i.e., public or private) was correlated with political ideology (Abbott, 1988) with social workers in public work settings tending to be more liberal than social workers in private settings. With regard to work experience, the more a social worker has, the more liberal their political ideology (Abbott, 1999). Finally, inconclusive evidence existed on the difference in political ideology by type of social worker function (i.e., administrators versus direct practice social workers) (Abbott, 1988).

POLITICAL IDEOLOGY AND PRACTICE EFFECT

A relationship was found between political ideology and clinical practice, namely that political ideology biases social workers. In an Israeli study, Lev-Wiesel and Friedlander (1999) learned that the majority of social workers have difficulty intervening with clients whose political ideologies differ from their own political ideologies. Another study suggested that social workers' personal bias and religiosity affected their attitudes on euthanasia and assisted suicide (Csikai, 1999). In a study that explored female child welfare workers, social workers held a bias for favoring mothers in child custody decisions (Sagi & Dvir, 1993). These studies are consistent with Linzer's (1999) discussion that social workers' difference in political ideology with clients can affect their practice.

Upon reviewing the literature before Rosenwald (2006a; 2006b) and Rosenwald and Hyde's (2006) research, the information on the political ideology of social workers appeared

RESEARCH ON POLITICAL DIVERSITY AND SOCIAL WORK

fragmented and tangential. Very few relevant studies used the actual term *political ideology*, and relevant studies had to be scanned for content that could be conceptually placed under its broad umbrella. No comprehensive literature review on the topic was found; the closest was Abbott (1988), who reviewed literature on the related areas of values. Furthermore, no theorist commonly appeared in the literature, and the theory's inclusion itself was sporadic.

The literature was tangential for two reasons. First, political ideology tended to be examined as an independent variable, measured by one item and serving as but one correlate in a larger research question. As a correlate, it measured the liberal and conservative continuum by ignoring New Left and New Right political ideologies. Second, political ideology of social workers appeared to be a little-studied topic; it was rarely the central focus of the study. Though political ideology itself appeared to be a fairly well-studied phenomenon based on the existing measures in the general population and in other academic disciplines, such as political science and sociology, it was not evident in the social work literature.

Minimal research in social work existed on political ideology's correlations with demographic and professional characteristics for two reasons. Although political ideology served alongside other correlates (e.g., race, degree) in exploring dependent variables, the relationship between political ideology and other correlates tends not be to be examined. Additionally, some studies correlated political ideology with other variables, but there the social workers were but one component of the sample and not singled out to hypothetically state, for example,

RESEARCH ON POLITICAL DIVERSITY AND SOCIAL WORK

that more conservative social workers tended to have more education than liberal social workers.

These limitations included a number of questions that warranted examination. Two of these were political ideology's relationship to professional affiliation and political ideology's effect on practice. With respect to professional affiliation as measured by professional participation, only two studies examined political ideology and professional participation (Epstein, 1969; Reeser & Epstein, 1990). In these studies, political party affiliation was the only measure of political ideology. Furthermore, no studies were found that explicitly examined political ideology's effect on practice. Several studies examined how social workers' values influence practice (e.g., Csikai, 1999; Rubinstein, 1994; Sagi & Dvir, 1993). As discussed, values do relate to political ideology. However, these studies examined social workers' views on particular social issues rather than a more complete representation of their total political ideology. Finally, no studies examined the confluence of these variables, that is, between demographic and professional correlates of political ideology, professional affiliation, and practice effect.

RECENT SCHOLARSHIP

In the first comprehensive study focused centrally on political ideology and social work, Rosenwald (2006a; 2006b) and Rosenwald and Hyde (2006) conducted a cross-sectional, random survey of 294 licensed social workers in a mid-Atlantic state. They used a forty-three-item revised version of Abbott's (1988)

• 73 •

RESEARCH ON POLITICAL DIVERSITY AND SOCIAL WORK

Professional Opinion Scale, which measured professional values linked to the policy statements from NASW's *Social Work Speaks* (2021),[2] as well as a seven-point, self-reported Likert Scale of political ideology (adapted from Knight [1999]) to measure social workers' political ideology. The participants' self-reported political ideologies, in descending order and rounded percentages, were liberal (41 percent), moderate (34 percent), very liberal (13 percent), conservative (10 percent), radical left (2 percent), very conservative (1/ percent), and radical right (0 percent) (Rosenwald, 2004). Furthermore, political party and political ideology as well as "other" spiritual affiliation and work status were related to political ideology. Those who identified as Democrat, Independent, other spiritual/religious affiliation, and worked full-time were more liberal than Republican, Protestant, and part-time social workers. These four variables explained 37.6 percent in political diversity. Overall, social workers were most liberal on their views of individual freedom and social responsibility. Furthermore, the findings "confirm Brint's (1994) conclusion that social workers tend to be more liberal on social issues than economic issues" (Rosenwald, 2006a, p. 124). For example, "social workers tended to be more liberal when welfare was needed to help with an unexpected crisis (that is, disaster, disability) and more moderate to conservative when advocating for clients on welfare to have fewer children and to record those who 'commit fraud'" (Rosenwald, 2006a, p. 124).

In Rosenwald's (2006b) study using the same dataset, a correlation existed between political ideology and professional affiliation ("fit" with the profession using NASW as a professional anchor). In this analysis, more liberal social workers felt more

RESEARCH ON POLITICAL DIVERSITY AND SOCIAL WORK

aligned to the profession while those who identified as more conservative felt slightly more marginalized professionally. In addition, more conservative social workers connected with a weaker belief in the Code of Ethics (Rosenwald, 2006b). Finally, social workers who were more liberal felt that holding a liberal ideology was essential to be a social worker (Rosenwald, 2006b).

In this same study (Rosenwald, 2006b), participants provided written comments and two themes emerged: diversity and representation. Regarding diversity, "the majority of participants who responded believed that a broad range of political ideologies should be reflected in social work" (p. 68). One participant wrote, "There should be no ideological litmus test [for the profession]" and another wrote, "With age, I have moved from liberal bleeding heart to moderate. I still serve our profession well" (pp. 68–69). Others were skeptical that social workers could be social workers and *not* liberal. For example, one participant stated, "By learning about social policy and inequalities that exist in society, an intelligent person may find it difficult to avoid becoming liberal" while another said, "It helps to have empathy [working in social work]. If one is too far to the right, there goes the empathy" (p. 69). There were challenges to this skepticism. For example, one participant stated, "Many 'liberal' views work against client empowerment and personal responsibility. Certain views assist clients to remain dependent and weak" and a second reported, "You don't have to be liberal to care" (p. 70).

Regarding the representation theme—that is, how strongly participants believed NASW represented them—participants' views on representation were mixed (Rosenwald, 2006b). They cited NASW's ability to legislatively advocate for social work

■ 75 ■

RESEARCH ON POLITICAL DIVERSITY AND SOCIAL WORK

values and match their political agenda (Rosenwald, 2006b). Yet, some participants believed that NASW was both too conservative—and too liberal, respectively. One participant wrote, "I dropped my membership last year. [NASW] needs to be a more radical [left] organization [and] inspire more activism among its members," while another stated "NASW is very liberal in its platform ideology (e.g., abortion, women's right to choose); my religious convictions are counter to the spirit of NASW. . . . I don't believe any discrimination is right; however, I see homosexuality as a choice—which is a sin in God's eyes. NASW seems to validate a homosexual lifestyle as okay, one not to be discriminated against—I have a problem with this" (Rosenwald, 2006b, p. 71).

Rosenwald and Hyde (2006) drew on the same aforementioned dataset and found a statistically significant relationship between social workers' political ideology and impact on practice. Findings included social workers believed they could separate their political ideology from the social work practice; in those situations where they could not, liberal social workers reported a reliance on use of their ideologies in practice more than conservative social workers. Finally, using the same dataset, Smith-Osborne and Rosenwald (2009) examined the relationship between religion and political ideology and found a small relationship existed between political ideology and both religious affiliation and religiosity.

Rosenwald (2006a; 2006b) and Rosenwald and Hyde's (2006) studies contributed to the literature on political ideology and social work in the following ways. They helped establish a literature on social workers and their political ideology,

· 76 ·

RESEARCH ON POLITICAL DIVERSITY AND SOCIAL WORK

located political ideology as the central focus of research, and examined a variety of demographic and professional correlates of political ideology. They also expanded on Fisher et al.'s (2001) recommendation to explore the relationship between political ideology (beyond political party identification) and professional affiliation. Finally, they probed the relationship between political ideology (beyond a particular political view) and effect on practice (Csikai, 1999, Deber et al., 1990; Fisher et al., 2001).

Since Rosenwald (2006a; 2006b) and Rosenwald and Hyde's (2006) work, additional studies were found in which the examination of political ideology was a central focus, as well as an array of studies and conceptual articles that examined social work students and practitioners' political ideology as a correlate of social workers on a particular social policy or advancing a particular ideology on a social policy. The studies all examined social work students with respect to political ideology and social work education. Flaherty et al. (2013) and Ringstad (2014) examined this area broadly while three others examined the relationship to political ideology and social work activism and political social work (Mizrahi & Dodd, 2013; Dodd & Mizrahi, 2017; Ostrander et al., 2017). Other studies brought up ideas to research political ideology (e.g., Dessel & Rodenborg, 2017b) though this was not the focus of the study.

POLITICAL DIVERSITY AND
SOCIAL WORK EDUCATION

Flaherty et al. (2013) examined the political climate in the classroom with a survey of social work students. They surveyed

RESEARCH ON POLITICAL DIVERSITY AND SOCIAL WORK

497 BSW and MSW students from ten social work programs. Almost half of the sample identified as Democrat, 23 percent as Independent, 14 percent as Republican, and 8 percent other (45 percent not Democrat). Conservative students found the social work classroom did not allow for open debate with students with different political ideologies. Flaherty et al. (2013) explain, "There was a significant trend for conservative students to be more likely to perceive harsh treatment in the classroom, to be more reluctant to express what they knew would be politically unpopular opinions, and to view the classroom as being less conducive to such discussion" (p. 67). These students referenced this discrimination, based on their own conservative view, in the classroom. When asked if there should be any disqualifying view that would be grounds to withhold a degree, only expressing explicit racism was identified.

Ringstad (2014) examined political ideology of social work students and drew on Abbott's (1988) Professional Opinion Scale. Surveys were completed by 127 MSW students (three cohorts). The political party affiliation breakdown included Democrats (55.9 percent), Republican (9.4 percent), Independent (7.9 percent), no party affiliation (19.7 percent), and other (2.45 percent) (Ringstad, 2014). Ringstad (2014) found that "political views do differ on sense of social responsibility based on political party. . . . No evidence was found that . . . political ideology changed during students' time in the educational program" (p. 13). Interestingly, participants' ethnicity was related to social responsibility. African Americans were the most liberal on this domain whereas Native American participants were neutral; Democrats were the most liberal on social responsibility and Republicans and Independents held the least liberal views.

Ringstad (2014) provides an important reflection:

> Overall, the results of this study lend support to the idea that social work is a liberal profession although results would indicate moderately liberal rather than very liberal views among participants. Similarly, while most scores were in the liberal range, a full third of participants could be more accurately described as moderate, calling into question the assumption that the social work profession is a liberal monolith and supporting the idea that a range of views are tolerated by the profession. Similarly, as all participants in this study were students enrolled in a graduate level social work education program, results appear to indicate social work students have fairly liberal views overall. Little evidence exists, however, that these liberal views are the result of the educational program. Rather, results may more accurately reflect who chooses to come to social work education rather than what social work education does to students. Two-thirds of the student participants in this study scored in the liberal range, one-third in the moderate range, and none in the conservative range on overall political ideology, and beginning and advanced students reported few differences in their political views. . . . In any case, participants in the current study reported more liberal views than found in prior research, and did so at the time of entering the profession

RESEARCH ON POLITICAL DIVERSITY AND SOCIAL WORK

(at the beginning of their educational program). These results do not support the idea that the social work professional standards or social work educational programs coerce individuals into liberal views. (p. 20)

POLITICAL DIVERSITY AND SOCIAL WORK STUDENT ACTIVISM

In Mizrahi & Dodd's (2013) research on student activism, they interviewed an MSW cohort at orientation (n=255) and at graduation (n=160) and used a social activism scale. At graduation, the majority were liberal (54) followed by moderate (16), radical (left) (12), other (7) and conservative (7). They explored, in part, the relationship of political ideology as a predictor for student activism at graduation. They found "differences related to a radical political affiliation (radical) and method of practice (community organizing) remained at graduation" (Mizrahi & Dodd, 2013, p. 589) and concluded that "those with a radical political ideology were disproportionately predicting a future of social activism as Reeser and Epstein (1990) and Fisher et al. (2001) also reported" (p. 597). The authors remind readers that it is important "to separate political views from social activism activities for analysis, because activism can be in service of moderate and conservative ideologies" (Mizrahi & Dodd, 2013, p. 594).

In a subsequent broader study, the same authors (Dodd & Mizrahi, 2017) examined the relationship of "demographic factors and activism"—including political affiliation among social work students. They surveyed 1,143 MSW students (three cohorts at orientation and upon graduation) at a major university. Political affiliation was significant to activism prior to entering the MSW program; students who identified as radical (left) were more activist than liberal-identified ones, who in turn were more activist than conservative-identified students (Dodd & Mizrahi, 2017). These differences disappeared during students' tenure in the MSW program as well as into their post-graduation career (Dodd & Mizrahi, 2017).

In a related article, Ostrander et al. (2017) conducted a study of social work students from two schools on efficacy and engagement plans in political social work training and relationship to their interest in political social work. Seventy-five percent identified as Democrats and none identified as Republican. While they found a significant difference with this training curriculum's impact on social work student efficacy, their recommendations for future research included the application of a political scale to examine nuances in participants' political ideology and the relationship between ideology and activism (Ostrander et al., 2017, p. 273).

POLITICAL IDEOLOGY AS A CORRELATE ON SOCIAL WORK ATTITUDE TOWARD PARTICULAR SOCIAL POLICY

Morality and Life

Recent studies examined the integration of Brint (1994) and NASW's (2021b) conception of morality and issues relating to life.

In a study of social work students, students who identified with more conservative political ideology were more anti-abortion as well as less supportive of birth control (Begun et al., 2017). Students who espouse anti-abortion attitudes—and are more conservative—may believe their views trump a client's views on abortion (Winter et al., 2016). Ninety percent of social work students believed that abortion laws should not be stricter and 70 percent believed abortion should be available in all circumstances (Witt et al., 2022) (this study was conducted prior to the U.S. Supreme Court's ruling in *Dobbs v. Jackson Women's Health Organization*, which overturned *Roe v. Wade*).

Related to the death penalty, almost 70 percent of social work students chose a life imprisonment option instead of the death penalty option in nine vignettes (Kennedy & Tripodi, 2015). Approximately half of these students favored a sentence of "life with the possibility of parole," which suggests a rehabilitation value of incarceration (Kennedy & Tripodi). Finally, related to physician-assisted suicide, Gaston, Randall, & Kiesel (2018), a study of end-of-life social workers, 54 percent supported it.

Civil Rights

Brint (1994) conceptualized the civil rights dimension of political ideology, and this has been applied to NASW's (2021b) policy statements on civil rights in recent literature on social work attitudes toward civil rights. Examples include social workers' attitudes toward addressing racism, LGBT equity, and immigration.

RACISM AND POLICY

A link exists between liberal social workers and more positive racial attitudes (Danforth, Hsu & Miller, 2020). Social work students who were younger (e.g., millennials) and cited more knowledge of the civil rights movement believed that racial oppression existed (in contrast to a color-blind society) (Davis, 2019). A study found 73 percent of social workers and social work students believed reparations should be provided to African Americans as compensation for the legacy of slavery and institutionalized racism (Jones, McElderry, & Conner, 2022). In the same study, 68 percent believed these reparations can begin to address racial healing (Jones et al.). Moreover, Jacobs et al. (2021) argue for social workers to cultivate transformative justice in healing communities and question social work's historic allegiance with the police state and its social control function (Jacobs et al., 2021). By decentering the role of social work and authentically engaging the community, the community voice is elevated to catalyze positive, systemic change (Jacobs et al.). There is still much room for social work policy, clinical practice, and education to bolster their initiatives to increase the profession's role in combatting anti-Black racism (Gregory & Clary, 2022).

LGBT DISCRIMINATION AND POLICY

Social work students who were more liberal were more likely to believe that the old "don't ask, don't tell" military policy was not affirming to LGBT individuals and that same-sex couples had a right to legally marry (Dessel and Rodenborg, 2017b). Conservative social workers and social work students were less likely to accept LGBT policies; these policies included LGBT acceptance on discussion of policies including acknowledging the range of sexual orientation prior to high school in public education and transgender individuals using the restroom that matches their gender identity (Lennon-Dearing & Delavega, 2016). In this same study, conservatives were less likely to agree that social workers' responsibility was to cultivate an affirming milieu for LGBT individuals (Lennon-Dearing & Delavega, 2016).

A conceptual article by Timbers and Yancy (2021) asks Christian social workers to grapple with nontraditional notions of gender identity and the very real "impact of [the Affordable Care Act and other policies] on the length and quality of life for transgender and gender-diverse people. These policies include Christian-affirming policies regarding routine care and access to hormonal treatments and surgeries (Timbers & Yancy).

ANTI-IMMIGRATION STANCE AND POLICY

A student survey assessed their views on support for individuals who qualify as DACA (Deferred Action for Childhood Arrivals) and equity in state higher education (McPherson, Villarreal-Otálora, & Kobe, 2021). Specifically, the majority of respondents (83 percent) believed not providing access to all state schools was segregation (and 25 percent were unaware their own university discriminated (McPherson et al.). Conservative social workers were 156 percent more likely and moderate

RESEARCH ON POLITICAL DIVERSITY AND SOCIAL WORK

social workers 61 percent more likely than strongly liberal social workers to believe "immigrants have the same opportunities for success as U.S.-born citizens" (Park et al., 2022, p. 457). Additionally, almost one-third of the study's social work student participants believed structural discrimination was at work for immigrants (Park et al.).

HEALTH

Health as a component of political ideology, while not discussed by Brint (1994), is addressed in *Social Work Speaks* (NASW, 2021b). Regarding the COVID-19 pandemic, no studies were located that examined social workers' attitudes toward wearing masks and receiving vaccines. This search was conducted given the politicization of decisions regarding masks and vaccines. In a Finnish study, social workers experienced some conflict with each other with the degree of "seriousness" that some—though not all—experienced COVID (Saraniemi et al., 2022).

Examining a different component of health—use of medical cannabis—one study found a majority of U.S. social workers in their sample support medical cannabis for client use (Findley et al., 2021). Finally, expanding health to environmental health and stewardship, social work students displayed some moderate support for the environment and the overwhelming majority of the sample engaged in some environmental activity (e.g., recycling) (Chonody, Sultman & Hippie, 2020). Liberal political ideology and nonreligious affiliation were two of the variables supportive of increased support of the environment (Chonody et al.).

■ 85 ■

ECONOMIC SYSTEMS AND THE WELFARE STATE

Interestingly, when examining economic systems and social work attitudes in the literature, no recent studies were found regarding social work students' attitudes toward capitalism, socialism, or other economic systems that Brint (1994) referenced. Even when examining the responsibility of the welfare state, little was found. One study reported that social work students overall were more in agreement that poverty was attributable to structural over individual factors—and this attribution toward structure increased after completion of a social welfare policy course (Delavega et al., 2017).

This chapter reviewed the history of research on scholarship on political ideology from the 1950s to the present day. We will return in Chapter 7 to additional ideas to build on this existing scholarship.

Chapter Four

SOCIAL WORK EDUCATION
AND POLITICAL DIVERSITY

*Social work is not a politically neutral profession.
Its emphasis on advocacy for the least powerful among
us and commitment to diversity and client self-determination may even set us at odds with some religious and
political ideologies. The profession is not for everyone,
and some students who enter our programs may find that
they are unable to reconcile their personal beliefs with
the profession's values and mission. This reality, however,
should not be misconstrued as a license to bully students
who hold minority views on complex and controversial
issues of social justice. Personal growth is most likely to
occur in an atmosphere in which risks are encouraged and
reasoned debate is modeled. We, and other authors, have
been debating the question: Does social work education
discriminate against conservative students? Perhaps a
better question is: How can we, as social work educators,
create an atmosphere in which reasoned debate of ideas
is encouraged while remaining true to the values and
mission of the profession?*

(Flaherty et al., 2013, pp. 71–72)

IN THE epigraph to this chapter, Flaherty and colleagues provide us with much needed food for thought when considering
students who do not represent the liberal monolith—from the
right and from the left. To what extent do social work educators think about political diversity in the classroom? Do they

recognize that diversity of political thought exists there among both faculty and students? And given this recognition, should it exist? In other words, while social work students may range in their political beliefs, is there some political litmus test that students should pass, or should subscribe to, that earns them the title of social worker? What is the responsibility of the educator, the university, or the Council of Social Work Education on this matter?

These questions lead to a discussion of how to address political diversity in social work education. Ringstad (2014) found the majority of social work students identifying with liberal followed by moderate ideologies prior to entering their programs. Dodd and Mizrahi (2017) noted students' political affiliations as a predictor of activism before their enrollment. Given that students enter with political ideologies and the ethical profession addresses social justice, we can turn to the Educational Policy and Accreditation Standards (EPAS) (Council on Social Work Education, 2022) for particular guidance and to entertain a variety of scenarios of how political diversity manifests in an array of courses.

RELEVANCE OF EDUCATIONAL POLICY AND ACCREDITATION STANDARDS

Is there a place for political diversity in social work education? Rosenwald et al. (2012) stated that this diversity should be identified and addressed and CSWE's EPAS articulate what

SOCIAL WORK EDUCATION AND POLITICAL DIVERSITY

diversity should formally comprise in social work education (Council on Social Work Education, 2022). CSWE provides curricular mandates to social work programs, and in the past three of five versions, including the current one, diversity with respect to political belief or ideology is included in these curriculum standards (Council on Social Work Education, 2022).

Here is the required competency from the EPAS (Council on Social Work Education, 2022):

COMPETENCY 3: ENGAGE DIVERSITY AND DIFFERENCE IN PRACTICE

The dimensions of diversity are understood as the intersectionality of factors including but not limited to age, caste, class, color, culture, disability and ability, ethnicity, gender, gender identity and expression, generational status, immigration status, legal status, marital status, *political ideology* (emphasis added), race, nationality, religion and spirituality, sex, sexual orientation, and tribal sovereign status (p. 9).

What we take as a directive from these standards is that political ideology is drawn from human experience, shapes identity, and accepts political diversity as a legitimate variable. It is possible that liberal and conservative students can respect that each other's ideas exist. And before we forget that some social workers can be inclined to be suspicious of those with conservative and New Right views, those who are liberal can accept that New Left or/ progressive ideas can have merit as well.

SOCIAL WORK EDUCATION AND POLITICAL DIVERSITY

NASW's *Code of Ethics* (National Association of Social Worker, 2021a) references the importance of respect for political diversity; "social workers should not practice, condone, facilitate, or collaborate with any form of discrimination on the basis of . . . political belief" (n.p.). Though not the only code of ethics, it is the default ethical pillar that is used to undergird teaching in social work programs as attributed in the Council's EPAS (Council on Social Work Education, 2022).

POLITICAL DIVERSITY EXAMPLES
IN COURSEWORK

To begin this conversation, let us examine how political diversity can manifest in five traditional areas in the delivery of social work education with the acknowledgment that curricula are delivered in varying ways. We can recall Brint's (1994) model of the range of political diversity based on civil rights, welfare state issues, moral and military rights, and system commitments to provide context and direction.

Table 4.1 shows a sample of potential topics and issues in social work coursework based on varying political ideologies.

FIELD EDUCATION

As the signature pedagogy in social work education, field education occupies a singular place in which political diversity may appear at the forefront. As students prepare for and engage in working with clients for their first time in a social work role,

• 90 •

TABLE 4.1 Topics and Issues with Potential Divergent Student Ideological Views

	Field Education	Policy	Practice	Theory	Research
Egalitarianism and Basic System Commitment	Role of field placement in supporting/ challenging the economic system	Fairness of economic systems	Consideration of clients' needs based on the economic system	Role of functionalism, conflict theory, and critical race theory on fairness of resource distribution	Evidence of effectiveness of economic systems
Welfare State	Eligibility for financial assistance	Role of TANF and housing choice vouchers	Eligibility for financial assistance	Role of theory on explaining need for assistance	Evidence of financial assistance need and effectiveness
Civil Rights	Belief in legitimacy of civil rights	Affirmative action LGBTQ rights Undocumented immigrants Voting rights	Belief in legitimacy of civil rights	Role of theory in explaining need for civil rights	Evidence of civil rights inequities
Moral/Military	Belief in when life begins and ends	Reproductive rights Militarism Vaccine mandates	Belief in when life begins and ends Belief in receiving vaccines	Role of theory in explaining existence of life	Evidence of when and how life should begin and end

issues relating to potential value conflict and emergence of political diversity awareness can occur.

Diversity awareness is an integral component of field education, and it is crucial for the field instructor, liaison, and field staff to be aware of the two forms of political diversity in which students need instruction: political countertransference and political transference. Figure 4.1 presents the dynamics of both.

Political Countertransference

Political countertransference is a construct that is triggered by the potential harm that students believe may occur when they disagree with their clients' positions (e.g., on abortion or same-sex marriage). This disagreement of political ideology, this reaction, occurs when a student's value manifested in a policy (e.g., being pro-choice and anti-vaccine) differs from the client's

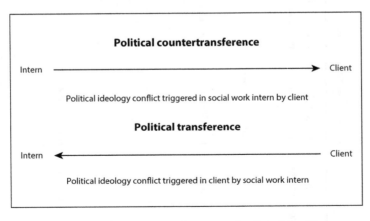

FIGURE 4.1 Political countertransference and political transference.

SOCIAL WORK EDUCATION AND POLITICAL DIVERSITY

(e.g., being pro-life and pro-vaccine). It is useful for students to become increasingly aware of their political ideology as it relates to *their reaction* to a client's presentation, which can refer to either the diversity inherent as a client's demographic characteristic or a particular political position as articulated by the client.

In the first scenario, consider the clinical presentation and how two students might vary. In this case, two students have clients who are undocumented immigrants. One student might believe that undocumented immigrants should be granted immunity while the other student believes that undocumented clients should be deported. In working with the clients, the value that emerges within the students with respect to the clients' immigration status suggests an awareness of political ideology that the student might not have previously been aware.

As an example of a client's articulated verbal expression, consider a client who reports that she is leaning toward having an abortion. Take these two social work students again—one is pro-life and one is pro-choice. The first student might have a much more challenging time, though not necessarily insurmountable, in working with this client. The second student, finding that this client's views on abortion are more similar to her own, finds such value congruence a refreshing component of their work together. This example provides a lens through which we can see how students in field education may react to a client based on client status or presentation or verbal expression.

Political Transference

Contrast that political countertransference with the scenario in which the client is triggered by some component of the social work intern's political ideology—the idea of *political transference*. Here, there is something triggering in the student's presentation or verbal expression that stimulates in the client a reaction that can be seen through a political ideological framework.

For the first example of presentation, assume that the client is non-Muslim and the social work intern is Muslim. The client is very suspect of Muslims in the United States and directly tells the student intern that he wants to be seen by a different intern who "belongs" in the country. Internally, the student is very shaken by the client's xenophobia, and she confides in her supervisor later that day. Here, a client's implicit disagreement with an intern on policy based on Muslim immigration showcases a transference on political ideology.

As a different example, with verbal expression as an indicator of political ideological divergence, consider the following scenario. A client seeks family therapy for himself and his teenage son, who is gay. The father wants the intern to align with the father's perspective that his son be "treated" so he becomes heterosexual. The intern, knowing full well NASW's statement on Sexual Orientation Change/Conversion Efforts (SOCE), which opposes such treatment on scientific grounds (National Association of Social Workers, 2015), is faced with the dilemma of how to respond to this client. This is another example of political transference being directed to the intern from the client.

SOCIAL WORK EDUCATION AND POLITICAL DIVERSITY

As students engage in their field experiences, their insight into their political countertransference, as well as their clients' political transference, will grow. From this insight, their professional development will mature. They will utilize and rely on their field educators and field liaisons for guidance in this domain. Certainly, not all encounters with clients will contain such issues, but preparing for this eventuality will prepare students to provide better assessment, intervention, and evaluation with their clients.

In sum, field education is the first opportunity for students in their professional development to engage with clients. It is also the first time for some, through formal social work education, that they may face and need to identify and negotiate these political value conflicts. Such value conflicts can manifest in all populations and practice settings where field education takes place.

PRACTICE COURSES

Practice courses—whether micro, mezzo, or macro in focus—provide the requisite academic knowledge and reflection for success in the field placement. They cover such components as intervention models, ethics and ethical decision making, diversity, and use of self. Political diversity is an essential component of this diversity, so attending to its presence and learning if and how to address it is part and parcel of professional education. Various ethical dilemmas based on values have long been part of the content in practice courses (Reamer, 2006; 2022), when these ethical dilemmas are grounded in political ideology, they

SOCIAL WORK EDUCATION AND POLITICAL DIVERSITY

become value differences reflecting political diversity. That is, framing these values based on policies is the link to the political diversity variable.

Not all value-based conflicts are based on policy, of course. A vignette in class might relate to how a student would feel if a client is consistently late. Another vignette could detail the debate of breaking confidentiality when an adolescent discloses drug use. It is the policy-driven values that are of interest to political diversity. Therefore, discussion in practice courses can attend to acknowledgement of political diversity, a discussion of the notion of "harm," as earlier referenced, and a course of action, including self-reflection and supervision, to find the best outcome for the client.

How do students' responses to micro, mezzo, and macro challenges—perceived "harm"—in practice when it comes to political diversity? What are the ethical implications at varying levels of practice? Let us examine this at three traditional levels of practice.

Micro level

As students discuss differences in political diversity with their clients in individual, family, and treatment group contexts, the aforementioned discussion of political transference and political countertransference can occur, particularly since political countertransference is a crucial component for students' professional development. How students identify, reflect, and respond to clients whose political ideology may differ from their own could have serious ethical implications for their clinical engagement.

SOCIAL WORK EDUCATION AND POLITICAL DIVERSITY

For example, we recall from previous studies cited that the vast majority of social work students are pro-choice (Witt et al., 2022). Assume a student who is pro-choice portrays a social worker in a role play in which her individual client is a sixteen-year-old who is pregnant and in foster care with limited support beyond her foster mother. This client would like to maintain her pregnancy and give birth to her child. The pro-choice student may think it is harmful to both the future mother and child when this is not the "best" time in the girl's life to have a child. To the extent that the student "pushes" her pro-choice values needs to be examined in class and discussed, as this is an example of the political countertransference that can occur in an actual practice setting. Conversely, in a reversed scenario in which the client is sixteen and wants to have an abortion, the student who is pro-life should become self-aware not to promote her own pro-life views. These two examples represent differing views on abortion and situate the students' views in thinking of harm, political countertransference, and political diversity.

While the previous example was in an individual context, the student should employ even greater care when learning about and role playing or simulating practice with couples, families, or treatment groups. This added caution stems from the larger number of clients within the identified treatment system, the reality that multiple political ideologies on a particular topic can manifest within a family or treatment group, and the emergence of varying political transferences. Using the same topic of family planning for a group of adolescent girls, the group leader needs to reflect on political countertransference as well as respond to potentially competing ideologies among members as well.

Mezzo level

As students participate in mezzo content—typically in their joint mezzo and macro coursework—they can engage in examining social welfare organizations' inherent political ideologies. These ideologies may be explicit or implicit and can be viewed in vision and mission statements as well as funding streams. For example, an agency that facilitates a patchwork of social welfare services for undocumented immigrants reflects a liberal to New Left ideology that may align—or not—with students' views on the extent that this population should be helped in the United States. As another example, students can examine funding streams at organizations and identify if financial investments are associated with funders with New Right or New Left values.

Finally, students can consider that if they serve one day as an executive director, for example, at an organization, to what extent their own political ideologies will align with their workplace. These discussions in class help students understand that alignment of political ideology with an agency for both field placement and future employment is a variable for consideration.

Macro level

Finally, at the community practice level, students can examine how their elected representatives—at the local, state, and federal levels—support or oppose the students' own political ideologies on a myriad of policy issues. As students learn about and

SOCIAL WORK EDUCATION AND POLITICAL DIVERSITY

eventually engage in legislative advocacy, support candidates' political campaigns, or seek elected office themselves, the classroom allows them to assess their ideology and the focus of their advocacy and political efforts with the existing political climate. That is, they can determine how much their political ideologies synchronize with these environments.

An additional consideration at the macro level is which entities under what circumstances are responsible for funding social welfare benefits. For example, more liberal students would support federal living-wage laws while more conservative students would favor private charities assisting clients who need financial assistance.

HUMAN BEHAVIOR COURSES

Human behavior courses focus on life stage models as well as sociological perspectives on human interaction. From a stage perspective, Erikson, Mahler, Piaget, Kohlberg, and other theorists introduce the tasks and expected milestones that individuals experience through development in their life span. With such an expansive view of human existence, policy-related issues can easily emerge. As human development is usually studied from cradle to grave, policies relating to conception and death bookend the course and can stimulate student discussion.

Regarding conception, questions of both reproductive rights and abortion are controversial. Students and instructors may have robust discussions on these topics. Furthermore, the field of genetic testing and engineering, in which parents have the

SOCIAL WORK EDUCATION AND POLITICAL DIVERSITY

ability to assess and make decisions on their fetus's health, can be quite provocative. On that topic, NASW states its "oppos[ition to] the use of genetic research to alter populations of people and to remove certain traits deemed by society as 'unfit'" (National Association of Social Workers, 2017, p. 143). With potential contentious subjects, the classroom provides the platform for such discussion. As we consider the end stage of life, heartfelt discussions relating to end-of-life care can occur. What is the role of euthanasia, as well as religion, in ending—or maintaining life? Do individuals have a right to have physician-assisted suicide, and what role does religion play in making such a decision? These topics are just a few examples of how political ideology—and its diversity—can manifest in human behavior courses that focus on human development.

For the sociologically oriented human behavior courses, the grand theories that are offered through functionalism, critical race theory, systems theory, Marxism, and postmodernism serve as a forum upon which we can see student and instructor political ideology converge and collide. Brint's (1994) "basic system commitments" might be most applicable here as society's organization of resource distribution and its attendant ability to achieve "social justice" can be critiqued and debated. Different macro theories emerge from different value assumptions about order, change, access to resources, and distribution of resources. Interestingly, the one distinctly claimed social work macro theory, systems theory, is silent on the social equity associated with change and end-state status (Robbins, Chatterjee, Canda, & Liebowitz, 2019).

SOCIAL WORK EDUCATION AND POLITICAL DIVERSITY

RESEARCH COURSES

Beyond the methodology-rich component of research courses, political diversity most manifests in the nature of the research question or hypothesis inquiry itself (Rosenwald et al., 2012). Regardless of study type, measure, or sample, the research question or hypothesis guides the entire research study. Therefore, what students select as their focus of study are reflections, in part, of their political ideologies.

Consider the following topic—Employment and Family Functioning—phrased as research questions from New Left, liberal, and New Right ideology perspectives.

- New Left: How does private-sector employment infringe on family stability?
- Liberal: How does the lack of a living wage infringe on family stability?
- New Right: How does women working outside of the home infringe on family stability?

Note that all three research questions have a consistent dependent variable—family stability—but the independent variables reflect typical questions from these three perspectives. The New Left perspective is extremely leery of the private sector to the extent that they believe it should not exist; the liberal perspective assumes that capitalism works but there needs to be a government-initiated living wage; and the New Right perspective assumes that the increase in women working in the

SOCIAL WORK EDUCATION AND POLITICAL DIVERSITY

workforce over the past decades has led to a decline in family functioning. This example shows the range of political ideologies, even in a research course, that can be seen within the nature of the inquiry. How an instructor chooses to accept a student's research question or hypothesis—and how fellow students may respond—is a classroom management issue that will be addressed later in the chapter.

POLICY COURSES

Certainly, social policy courses mostly reflect the political ideology—in course content, in instructor intention, and in student engagement. NASW's *Social Work Speaks* (National Association of Social Workers, 2021b), as referenced earlier, is the bible of the profession and encompasses dozens of policy statements relevant to political diversity. Child welfare policy, aging policy, affirmative action, the death penalty, and economic policy are just a few of the topics in which policy views reflective of different political ideologies emerge and are open for deliberation.

As an example, let us examine the minimum wage. While virtually all people across the spectrum believe in a minimum wage, what is the right amount for it? The federal hourly minimum wage of $7.25/hour is far lower than Seattle's $17.27 hourly rate. NASW (2021b) argues for a "federal minimum wage indexed to cost-of-living increases and [that] is a living wage" (p. 238). What is the correct "ceiling" for a minimum wage?

As another example, we can recall the COVID-19 pandemic and the resultant policies that required vaccines for certain

SOCIAL WORK EDUCATION AND POLITICAL DIVERSITY

public sector employment. If we think of body autonomy, that tenet is traditionally associated with liberal ideology and is used as a rationale for pro-choice as well as physician-assisted suicide arguments. Yet this body autonomy argument can be argued from a conservative perspective: individuals have a right to not have a vaccine injected in their bodies as a condition of employment. What is the right policy for public sector employees during a pandemic? Furthermore, this example suggests the political permeability of a rationale to make one's case.

Such issues will come up in policy courses, and the diversity of political ideology will most likely be shown by students. This debate can emerge in the context of a formal lecture, in-class debate, spontaneous discussion, reading response, or larger, written assignment. Faculty are left to field questions from students, including the popularity/stigma of aligning with different political views and the impact this has on their social work identity. The alignment with a political view will be on full display of the student's peers as well as the professor. The expression of view can also extend beyond the traditional liberal/conservative response to expressions of New Left/Progressive as well as New Right perspectives depending on the topic.

STRATEGIES TO ADDRESS CONFLICT OF POLITICAL DIVERSITY IN SOCIAL WORK EDUCATION

Having reviewed how political ideology—and its diversity—manifests in five content areas in social work education, we can focus on some strategies for addressing this diversity.

INCREASE INSTRUCTOR AWARENESS OF POLITICAL IDEOLOGY EXPRESSION

Perhaps the first strategy to consider is the degree to which an instructor is even aware that a political ideology has been expressed (Rosenwald et al., 2012). Faculty might believe they are neutral when in fact their very rhetoric, choice of instructional materials, required and supplemental readings, and guest speakers reflect an implicit political ideology. Therefore, their assessment and acceptance of their own political ideology, naming it, helps them identify an important aspect of the nature of their instruction.

Conversely, some faculty might purposely want to explicitly express their political ideology. In this case, to what extent do they reveal to students that they are speaking from a New Left—or conservative—political philosophy? Faculty who are this explicit with their political ideology should both acknowledge and share it with students in the spirit of full disclosure and subscription to a transparent pedagogical philosophy.

ENSURE ROOM FOR A RANGE OF POLITICAL IDEOLOGY EXPRESSIONS IN THE CLASSROOM

"Is There Room for One More?" is the subtitle of an article Rosenwald et al. (2012) wrote on political diversity in the classroom. It described the political diversity variable and its ability to be fully "present" in the social work classroom. Aside

SOCIAL WORK EDUCATION AND POLITICAL DIVERSITY

from the variable reflected in the strategy above—instructor acknowledgment—the fundamental issue comes to this: Do students feel "safe" expressing their political ideology regardless of its popularity in social work? Can a student who is conservative state that social work is wrong about abortion? Can a student who is New Left state that socialism is the answer instead of capitalism? As described earlier in the text, the "liberal" assumption of social work—confirmed by a number of authors, such as Flaherty et al. (2013)—has long been a safe haven in the classroom. This author has personally had a graduate social work student take him aside and state that as a Republican, she felt "closeted" in her social work experience. Therefore, creating these a refuge in the classroom is paramount.

MANAGE THE CLASSROOM EFFECTIVELY

Recognizing that instructors have their own political ideology and that students as a group have a range of political ideologies are important foundations for the third strategy—effective classroom management (Rosenwald et al., 2012). Hodge (2011) argues, "Progressive populations should be able to work with orthodox populations, within the boundaries of their personal values, and vice-versa" (p. 244). Five pedagogical principles cultivate a civil classroom environment: "(1) use common self-descriptors; (2) avoid ideological modifiers; (3) discuss populations in a fair, strengths-based manner; (4) present conflicting perspectives with equitable empathy; and (5) attend to power differentials" (Hodge, 2011, p. 244).

Therefore, setting a classroom tone in which all groups are discussed in a strengths-based and empathic manner is necessary though challenging. After all, when students or instructors feel strongly, giving respect to others' opinions might not be at the top of their list. Therefore, Hodge's (2011) recommendations provide a useful framework that guides initial conversations about political diversity. Adding a statement of group rules that include guidelines on respect and ensuring sufficient time for all participants can be added to this list.

EMPLOY PRACTICAL REFLECTIVITY

Reflectivity is the ability to engage in self-assessment on how one's values and ideas are formulated and presented (Yip, 2006). As Yip (2006) suggests (also talking about social work practice), practical reflectivity is challenging yet necessary in the classroom. The principles of practical reflectivity include 1) acknowledging it is an ongoing process; 2) examining students' learning and reflection; 3) recognizing the mutually engaging process for its occurrence; 4) understanding the gradated process to build comfort; and 5) cultivating the flexibility and multiple perspectives on thinking and feeling that coexisted (p. 253).

Imagine the skill and deftness of an educator in facilitating such reflectivity through these principles in the classroom. It is

SOCIAL WORK EDUCATION AND POLITICAL DIVERSITY

precisely this type of pedagogical stance that would set the stage for a true discussion of political diversity.

IMPLEMENT INTERGROUP DIALOGUE

With such conflicts that can occur in the classroom, an intergroup dialogue as intervention can be useful. These dialogues are group-based educational interventions that seek to reduce prejudice by engaging individuals with different belief systems and experiences in focused and extended discussion (Dessel & Rodenborg, 2017a; Gurin, Nagda & Zimena, 2013). Though they are traditionally focused on groups with respective histories of privilege and oppression that center on a certain social variable (e.g., race, sexual orientation), they can be useful in bringing together students with different political ideologies to have honest and sustained dialogues on their differences and perhaps find common ground. Dessel, Bolen, and Shepardson (2011) observed that intergroup dialogues can be very challenging as students' basic assumptions and stereotypes can be safely discussed and students' value systems are questioned. These observations on intergroup dialogues pertain to ones on political ideology as well. Intergroup dialogues are not easy to participate in nor are they quick fixes to reconcile divergent political beliefs. But their provision and emphasis in social work education has great potential to provide space for articulation, clarity, and compromise. These dialogues align with Hodge's (2011) recommendations.

TEACH AND APPLY ETHICAL DECISION MAKING

Examining political diversity through ethical decision making can be taught and applied throughout the social work curriculum for BSW, MSW, and PhD/DSW students. Two ethical components, self-determination and social justice, play a large role in how political diversity is formulated—and respected. Most students have formulated their views on achieving social justice policies prior to becoming a social work student (Dodd & Mizrahi, 2017). When they appear in a classroom together, it may be challenging to recognize that other students can self-determine their political ideologies. This is complicated when faculty teach NASW's agenda as the official agenda of the profession. Examining ethics in social work, Valutis, Rubin, & Bell (2012) observe "the conflict and congruence between personal and professional values and beliefs . . . suggestions for moral reasoning and ethical decision making in practice . . . and discussions of professional socialization and the teaching of ethical decision-making skills" (pp. 1046–1047)

The journey toward students' self-determination on their political ideologies begins prior to university admission, continues as they are socialized into NASW's policy statements, and continues, perhaps, after graduation. Socialization into the profession's ideology will happen for many, but others will emerge finding the profession too liberal, too conservative, or somewhere in between. Educators may need to accept that some graduating students collide with notions of social justice. To assist educators, a sample course syllabus devoted to political diversity and social workers is found in Appendix A; this syllabus can be used as a standalone elective or as part of a policy or diversity undergraduate or graduate course.

CULTIVATE CRITICAL THINKING

Promoting critical thinking with an analytical discussion of political ideology and its diversity is very useful in the classroom as it helps with power dynamics (Rosenwald et al., 2012). However, Reisch and Staller (2011) urge caution with oversimplification of political ideology and stereotyping:

> Governing faculties of schools of social work, and the students drawn to them, tend to associate themselves with liberal agenda-setters when it comes to identifying and solving individual and social problems. When these two phenomena are conflated, the result can be an over-simplified belief that liberalism promotes social justice and that conservatism impedes it. There are several hazards associated with teaching social policy courses structured along this ideological divide. First, it tends to assume a uniformity of views within a classroom that probably does not exist. Second, it builds on this assumed consensus by encouraging students to embrace positions to which they are already leaning. Third, it tends to encourage students to identify opposition in the positions of those held outside the classroom and school environment. Thus, it provides the means and the justification for simplifying the world into easily identified and reproduced categories of thought." (p. 133)

SOCIAL WORK EDUCATION AND POLITICAL DIVERSITY

Can social justice only be claimed by one ideological group? Probably not. While *Social Work Speaks* (National Association of Social Workers, 2021b) clearly identifies social justice goals—and routes to its attainment—others might have different routes, perhaps even different goals. And before simplifying this into the familiar liberal-conservative divide, consider that some on the New Left would strongly disagree with the "conservative" route of the liberal. This critique from the left was seen, for example, in the 2020 Democratic Party presidential primary. Senator Bernie Sanders, a self-proclaimed socialist, advocated for a single-payer health system while the more moderate candidate, Joe Biden, did not agree.

Consequently, educators must join with students and catalyze critical-thinking skills to help students clearly articulate their ideologies regardless of what they are. In discussing political diversity, Flaherty et al. (2013) argue for critical thinking and believe that its presence can coexist with the explicit policy routes and goals established by NASW.

> Educators must be cognizant of the immense power imbalance that exists between instructor and student and of how intimidating it can be to be in the minority, including the political minority. Students do not come to us as blank slates. They arrive with an array of strengths and limitations, skills and deficits, deeply held beliefs and tentatively held notions. They may be unprepared to articulately defend some ideas and may not have been previously challenged to do so. As social work educators, it is our responsibility to model critical reasoning and constructive debate and to promote

SOCIAL WORK EDUCATION AND POLITICAL DIVERSITY

a classroom atmosphere that encourages students to take intellectual risks while still adhering to the profession's commitment to social justice. In doing so, we must also be willing to defend our ideas and positions against reasoned challenges without resorting to dogma or intimidation. Social policy positions promoted by the NASW and the CSWE are rooted in ethical principles and scientific evidence and are defensible through appeals to the same. If we find ourselves unable to defend a particular sociopolitical position through these means, perhaps the position should be reexamined. Would not we expect the same from our students?" (pp. 70–71)

In fostering critical thinking, a question remains: Is the exchange of nonliberal ideologies a necessary, developmental exchange while students arrive at the truth of the policy statements in *Social Work Speaks* (National Association of Social Workers, 2021b). Or does the answer lie in something more profound: If socialization is not completely successful, will students graduate with political ideologies *across* the political spectrum?

CONCLUSION

The Council on Social Work Education requires that political diversity be fully honored in the classroom. It clearly manifests in a wide range of course content in the social work curricula. Multiple ways exist to address this ideology—from the instructor's perspective, from students' perspective, and from pedagogy used. Barsky, Sherman, and Anderson (2015) remind educators, "Moving forward, it is important to maintain open dialogue between social work educators, regardless of whether they take an evangelical, conservative, liberal, secular, humanistic, or other approach to teaching (Dessel, Bolen & Shepardson, 2011). Educators should resist closing discussion on issues simply because such discussions might be difficult, emotional, or challenge core aspects of their religious and social identities" (p. 86).

As we consider this newer variable that is emerging in the social work classroom, we need to learn to welcome its presence.

Chapter Five

POLITICAL IDEOLOGY AND SOCIAL WORK PRACTICE

*I do occasionally express my views briefly if an issue
arises in therapy which I see as . . . potentially harmful to
others (e.g., racial discrimination) but I do not get into a
power struggle.*

(Rosenwald & Hyde, 2006, p. 17)

*My political views are informed by my Christian
identity—by the Bible so the issue is more how do I handle differences between what I believe in the Bible and
the beliefs/political views of my clients, agency, etc.. . . .
If there is a time when my beliefs will negatively impact
my practice (i.e., with a homosexual client), I will refer
them to someone with that expertise.*

(Rosenwald & Hyde, 2006, p. 19)

THESE ARE but two examples of real practice examples in which
social work practitioners discussed political ideology in their
practice (Rosenwald & Hyde, 2006). Given that social workers
recognize that they have a political orientation, we can pose
a number of questions: To what extent do workers recognize
they have a political ideology? To what extent does it mirror
(or not) the profession's policy statements? To what extent does
it manifest in practice? Is it addressed? Should it be addressed?
If so, how?

These questions set the stage to examine the practice setting in relation to political diversity. In this chapter, we examine the manifestation of political diversity in practice and how to address it with specific methods. Accompanying vignettes provide examples of tension that can be impacted by political diversity.

POTENTIAL IMPACT OF POLITICAL IDEOLOGY ON PRACTICE

Beyond examination as a diversity variable in its own right, the manifestation of political diversity is applicable because of the social work profession's applied nature. Political ideology, like all other aspects of a social worker's experience, education, and biography, are brought into the clinical encounter. As practitioners engage with clients, as well as with agencies, and interface with agency policy, they may or not be aware of the influence of their values associated with positions on policy issues. Recall from chapter 1 the numerous stances that one may have on various policy positions. Depending on how conscious or not they are of their policy positions that *are* their values, social workers have greater or lesser awareness of the role and dimension of political ideology that they bring to their professional practice. As referenced, Rosenwald and Hyde (2006) found that political ideology impacts practice to some degree and, therefore, social workers need to have greater awareness of this impact.

Why should we study political ideology in practice? Let us examine this first on a micro-level. As a diversity variable that has not been fully or empirically examined, it "fits" into analysis of a practitioner's awareness of self. We return to the concept of political countertransference introduced in chapter 4.

POLITICAL COUNTERTRANSFERENCE REVISITED

To review, *political countertransference* is the dynamic in which a social worker's emotions and thoughts are of a policy nature and, therefore, reflect political ideology. In other words, it relates to the practitioner's affective and cognitive response to a client's presenting issue that triggers a policy response. Indeed, the role of emotion in policymaking is established (Westen, 2007). Consider clients' presenting issues, including clients who are undocumented immigrants, clients who are LGBTQ, and clients who are interested in family planning. In these examples, the social worker may strongly believe that undocumented immigrants should not even be residing in the United States or that LGBTQ individuals should not have children either through surrogacy or adoption. Consider clients considering vaccines, physician-assisted suicide, or being just over the income eligibility for federal or state benefits. All of these issues may appeal to the social worker's ideology and compel them to act—either in congruence with the client's wishes or as a counterreaction to the client's needs.

From their education onward, social workers are encouraged to engage in reflectivity to identify any conscious (or subconscious) values that might impact the clinical encounter (Yip, 2006). After all, clients are typically in vulnerable life situations and think of and rely on social workers as "authorities" in their (clients') lives.

Examining political countertransference is vital to sound professional practice and is an ongoing professional development function of practitioners. Becoming aware of their positions on policies that might impact their practice is essential for ethical practice. If a social worker feels very strongly that abortion is illegal in all circumstances—or that the Temporary Assistance for Needy Families (TANF) program's eligibility rules are too strict, they need to have an awareness and an ability to reflect on what—if anything—should be shared in practice and in supervision. They might want to express their views through a "recommendation" to a client who is uncertain and vulnerable. Even more so, there is a risk that social workers will unduly persuade a client, for example, to have an abortion—or not—or to lie about welfare eligibility to secure TANF funding to offset a corrupt capitalistic system.

AN ETHICAL FRAMEWORK FOR UNDERSTANDING POLITICAL DIVERSITY IN PRACTICE

Value conflicts in social work have been discussed in social work for over fifty years (Varley, 1968; Linzer, 1999; Reamer, 2022; Barsky, 2022). As political ideology is framed as a value that social workers hold on a variety of policy positions, such value conflicts manifest in ethical dilemmas that arise based on disagreement in political ideologies or, in other words, political diversity. Conflicts rooted in varying political ideologies present

POLITICAL IDEOLOGY AND SOCIAL WORK PRACTICE

an interesting challenge to social workers as they can impact clinical relationships as well as organizational and macro practice. Value conflicts can abound in practice and can be perceived as ethical dilemmas. Reamer (2022) writes, "There is no simple, tidy formula for resolving ethical dilemmas. By definition, ethical dilemmas are complex. . . . Reasonable, thoughtful social workers can disagree about the ethical principles and standards that ought to guide ethical decisions in any given case."

An ethical framework is essential to practice as it guides practitioner-client boundaries, provides moral concepts that anchor practice, and suggests a path forward in assessing an intervention. The framework introduced in chapter 4 is more fully presented as a tension between two key, yet competing, ethical values: self-determination (as part of the dignity and worth of the person) and social justice (National Association of Social Workers, 2021a). The central tension between competing ethical standards should be examined to provide insight into how conflicts among political ideology can arise. This examination asks the broader question—can political diversity exist in social work practice? We will return to this question shortly.

Self-determination is a component of the value of "dignity and worth of the person" and is included in its ethical principle: "Social workers respect the inherent dignity and worth of the person. Social workers treat each person in a caring and respectful fashion, mindful of individual differences and cultural and ethnic diversity. Social workers promote clients' socially responsible self-determination (National Association of Social Workers, 2021c)". Honoring self-determination is a hallmark of social workers' engagement with clients. It is central to a host of psychotherapies, case management, and client-centered advocacy.

Social justice is a long-standing value of the social work profession. The NASW *Code of Ethics* (2021a) identifies social justice as a value and states it as an ethical principle: "*Social workers challenge social injustice.* Social workers pursue social change, particularly with and on behalf of vulnerable and oppressed individuals and groups of people. Social workers' social change efforts are focused primarily on issues of poverty, unemployment, discrimination, and other forms of social injustice."

We can think of social justice in its most common form as "distributive justice" (Hoefer, 2019; Rawls, 1971). Rawls (1971) introduces social institutions' organization of "distributive shares" that warrant the "appropriate distribution of the benefits and burdens of social cooperation" (p. 4). Hoefer (2019) succinctly examines the core of social justice as the core of the redistribution of resources—income, civil rights, and the like—that originated with Rawls's (1971) political philosophy. Hoefer (2019) references the challenge of interpreting distributive justice for what may be considered an equitable distribution of resources to one is seen quite differently by another.

These varying views Hoefer (2019) alludes to reflect the very political nature of the conflict that can manifest in the clinical encounter. Furthermore, from the perspective of political ideology diversity, we can think of social justice "challenging" self-determination both from the left and the right. In practice, when a social worker's political ideology is congruent with

POLITICAL IDEOLOGY AND SOCIAL WORK PRACTICE

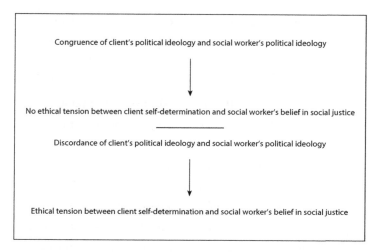

FIGURE 5.1 Political ideology and competing ethical principles.

any manifested political ideology of the client, the tension does not exist. But when a client's presentation challenges the social worker's political ideology, the social worker's reliance on the client's self-determination over their own sense of social justice is challenged. This tension between the two ethical principles is depicted in figure 5.1.

THE PERCEIVED NOTION OF HARM

As introduced in chapter 3, the fulcrum on which these ethical tensions balance is the concept of harm. All social workers agree that self-determination should be violated when a client is suicidal or homicidal or is perpetuating child or elder maltreatment.

This is because there is imminent risk or actual evidence of harm. Broadening this concept, the notion of harm is useful to analyze why the aforementioned tension between self-determination and social justice occurs. Rosenwald and Hyde (2006) describe a study that included the effect of political ideology on practice and introduced this concept of harm.

> In terms of criteria, the prevention of "harm" was a crucial factor in expressing or acting on one's political ideology. In this case, "harm" was understood as an action or potential action that threatens some aspect of social justice. Social justice, in turn, often is informed by one's political ideology. Therefore an "unjust" or "harmful" act, as viewed through a particular ideological lens, needs to be challenged or addressed. One dilemma, however, is that "harm" for one person may not so for another. This can result in a conflict between worker and client around such issues as expressing racism, sexist or homophobic language; abortion as an option for an unwanted pregnancy; or dependence on welfare benefits. Such conflict has the potential to erode the practitioner-client relationship. (p. 20)

What makes a social worker decide to violate a client's self-determination? Specifically, it can occur if any tension comes from the social worker perceiving that a client's presenting issue somehow violates the distribution of resources per distributive justice (Hoefer, 2019). Distributive justice allocates resources—civil rights, cash assistance, housing vouchers—in a particular pattern in society by legislative, executive, or judicial activity (Hoefer, 2019; Reisch, 2018). When the social worker believes and values, as represented by their political ideology, that a resource should be allocated in a different manner than the client believes—or of which the client is even consciously aware—this may pose an ethical dilemma based on political ideology. For example, a social worker might believe that a client who is espousing a racist belief is harming because of unchecked racist stereotypes (most social workers believe that racial oppression exists [Jones, McElderry, & Conner, 2022]). From a liberal perspective, the social worker might challenge this client to become aware of and rethink this prejudice. In another example, from a conservative perspective, a social worker who is working with a client who is considering a vaccine might challenge the client about harming her body even though the federal policy promotes vaccines.

If the worker and the client are in sync with their policy positions, then no tension exists between them. It is only when there is a disagreement (or even a strong inference of disagreement) by the social worker that tension exists as well as the perception that harm may occur.

ETHICAL DILEMMAS INVOLVING POLITICAL DIVERSITY

We turn to some examples that represent the range of Brint's (1994) conception of ideology in four vignettes (moral/military issues, civil rights, welfare state, egalitarian and basic system commitment) (see table 5.1).

POLITICAL IDEOLOGY AND SOCIAL WORK PRACTICE

TABLE 5.1 Practice Examples of Ethical Conflicts Based on Political Diversity

Moral/Military Force	Civil Rights	Welfare State	Egalitarianism and Basic System Commitment
End-of-life decision making and care	Immigration eligibility	Welfare benefit eligibility	Patriarchy and gendered employment

Each of the four vignettes is followed by a discussion of harm and a discussion of the attendant policy statement from *Social Work Speaks* (National Association of Social Workers, 2021b). We will view these vignettes with scenarios from several different political ideologies to illustrate value differences based on political diversity.

VIGNETTE #1

A social worker is working with a 90-year-old client who has end-stage renal failure. The client is in home hospice and resides in a state that has physician-assisted suicide (PAS). The client does not want morphine for the pain because she wants to only enjoy quality time with her daughter and grandchildren. Her days are becoming increasingly filled with pain.

Scenario 1 (Liberal Perspective): The social worker supports PAS, and when informing the client about this state policy, the client states immediately that she does not want to hear more as it violates her religious beliefs. The social worker educates the client on the options and then advocates for PAS as a "moral" issue so the client is not in pain.

Scenario 2 (Conservative Perspective): The social worker believes PAS is immoral but the client strongly wants to consider it. On moral grounds, that everyone should die a "natural" death, the social worker tries to dissuade the client.

Harm is seen here from two different perspectives. From the liberal perspective, the client who does not want to even consider hearing about PAS may be premature in her thinking and harming herself. From the conservative perspective, the client who wants to seriously consider PAS even though the social worker is against it is harming herself by ending her life artificially.

On the topic "End-of-Life Care and Decision Making," *Social Work Speaks* (National Association of Social Workers, 2021b) promotes "consumer education and health care practitioner communication about the full range of options for end-of-life care and the potential benefits and risks associated with each option" and "[the] client's ability to exercise the full range of legally available options as the end of life approaches" (p. 104). Himchak (2011) discusses the social justice perspective relating to PAS among senior populations. This vignette, and the context in which political diversity can manifest, presents as a value conflict over moral issues and political diversity.

VIGNETTE #2

A social worker is working in foster care and trying to find a relative for a child so that that child does not enter foster care. The one

relative who is found locally is undocumented. While the relative
successfully passed a background check and home visit, the worker
is wondering if this kinship care placement would be feasible due
to the relative's immigration status.

Scenario 1 (Liberal Perspective): The social worker agrees to keep the relative's undocumented status concealed as creating a kinship care placement is in the best interest of the child.

Scenario 2 (Conservative Perspective): The social worker believes that because undocumented workers reside in the United States illegally, this relative does not deserve to be a guardian, and moreover, the instability of the documentation status wouldn't make this placement feasible for the child. The relative is very willing to serve as a guardian, but the social worker is leery.

Again, harm is seen from two different perspectives. From the liberal perspective, the social worker is willing "to do what is necessary" regarding authorizing the placement in the best interest of the child; failure to ensure this placement would harm the child by denying the child an otherwise stable kinship care placement. From the conservative perspective, the social worker believes that the relative being here illegally is wrong; therefore, they believe the relative would not be a good role model for the child. Additionally, there are safety concerns about the relative possibly being deported.

On the topic "Immigrants and Refugees," *Social Work Speaks* (National Association of Social Workers, 2021b) promotes "uphold[ing] and support[ing] equity and human rights for immigrants and refugees, while at the same time protecting

POLITICAL IDEOLOGY AND SOCIAL WORK PRACTICE

national security" (p. 179; see also McPherson, Villarreal-Otálora & Kobe, 2021). This vignette illustrates the "human right" for the relative to be considered as a viable kinship care placement.

This discussion on civil rights is a hallmark of political ideology and an occasion where conflict can occur. In this example, a conflict with the social worker and the "system" would work against the client becoming a kinship caregiver.

VIGNETTE #3

A social worker is working with a client who is a waiter and who has been struggling financially. After a careful review of the client's income and expenses, the social worker determines that client earns $500 over the ceiling to receive benefits from the Supplemental Nutrition Assistance Program for a family of one.

Scenario 1 (New Left Perspective): The social worker believes that the capitalist system "rigs" basic needs for many and, therefore, believes that while it's only a temporary solution, recommends to the client to not report $500 in tips. The client does not want to lie.

Scenario 2 (Liberal/Moderate/Conservative Perspective): The social worker is empathetic with the client that his income is too high but will not commit welfare fraud. The client pleads with the social worker to support him in his application, but the social worker states he will review the client's application for accuracy if it is submitted for review.

Here, harm is seen from two different perspectives. From the New Left perspective, the harm applies to the client, who is

POLITICAL IDEOLOGY AND SOCIAL WORK PRACTICE

forced to work in an economic system that does not provide a fair wage. What might be construed as fraud by many is actually helping to level the playing field. The client is more liberal than New Left and does not agree with the social worker's recommendation. On the other hand, from a liberal to conservative perspective, the worker is honest and will not make this recommendation. The client, more New Left, does not believe it is fair that the system is so stacked against him.

On welfare reform, *Social Work Speaks* (National Association of Social Workers, 2021b) promotes "policies that protect the entitlement status of Medicaid and food stamps for all who meet eligibility criteria, including immigrants, refugees, and noncitizens" (p. 318). When considering that the poverty threshold for an individual is $19,320 a year or $1,610/month (2022 data), the emotional weight that presents itself to the social worker—to ignore or to advocate with—becomes apparent. Note that this vignette is different from the first two vignettes because the critique of the official *Social Work Speaks*'s position—here on welfare reform eligibility—is from the left.

VIGNETTE #4

A social worker is working with a couple in couples counseling. Mr. D is the service director at a car dealership while Mrs. D is a part-time housekeeper at a local motel and primarily raises their three children. In counseling, the couple agrees that Mr. D has the more important job as he brings home ten times Mrs. D's salary. For one session, the social worker asks to check-in with each individual separately, to which they agree. When talking to

POLITICAL IDEOLOGY AND SOCIAL WORK PRACTICE

the social worker, Mrs. D. continues to share that her husband's work is more important than hers.

Scenario 1 (Liberal Perspective): The social worker is a proponent of caregiving as unpaid work and challenges Mrs. D to consider raising children qualifies as such. This is very surprising to Mrs. D, and she disagrees with the social worker.

Scenario 2 (Conservative Perspective): The social worker reflects on Mrs. D's statement and asks her what she means (though does not recognize her unpaid work as equal in status to paid work). Mrs. D believes that childrearing and working part-time are just as important as Mr. D's work.

Here, harm is seen from two different perspectives. From the liberal perspective, the social worker believes that it is harmful not to empower Mrs. D and informs her that unpaid work is indeed work. From the conservative perspective, the social worker empathizes with Mrs. D.; she (the social worker) was raised to think that it is the man's role to bring home the greater income in a relationship and has a traditional sense of labor as paid labor.

On the topic "Women's Issues," *Social Work Speaks* (National Association of Social Workers, 2021b) promotes "conceptualizing caregiving as work because 30 percent of adults, most of who are working women, annually serve as unpaid caregivers . . . ; these women should be valued socially, legally, and economically" (p. 336). Indeed, "women perform two thirds of unpaid caregiving work. The enormous demands of unpaid work reduce many women's opportunities to participate fully in the paid workforce" (Reid & LeDrew, 2013, p. 81). This vignette and the context in which political diversity can manifest as a value conflict over patriarchy and gendered employment and displays yet another issue relating to political ideology and diversity.

STRATEGIES TO ADDRESS VALUE CONFLICTS IN CLINICAL PRACTICE BASED ON POLITICAL DIVERSITY

Having explored the manifestation of political ideology in clinical practice, we have also reviewed when tensions in political diversity can result in a value conflict. We now turn to some strategies to address these conflicts and resolve them—or prevent them from occurring in the first place—from a clinical perspective.

IDENTIFYING POLITICAL COUNTERTRANSFERENCE

As described earlier, political countertransference can manifest, like all dimensions of countertransference, in the therapeutic relationship. Given that the relationship is paramount to all therapeutic encounters, an awareness of this type of countertransference is warranted. Social workers need to accept that, like all individuals, they have values associated with policy positions that may impact their understanding and perspective. This impact can occur based on working with clients as well as the context of clients' circumstances. For example, careful consideration would prompt social workers to scan their own psyches and evaluate whether a particular political ideology on a certain

POLITICAL IDEOLOGY AND SOCIAL WORK PRACTICE

policy position is unduly influencing their work, or potential work, with a client. Woodcock (2008) advises that social workers become more aware of their political philosophy. Such an examination of political countertransference's presence is sound social work practice.

UTILIZING PRACTICAL REFLECTIVITY
AND USE OF SELF

As discussed in chapter 4, practice reflectivity helps social workers engage in a full examination of political countertransference (Yip, 2006). "Critical reflection . . . transforms practice by challenging the existing social, political and cultural conditions and structural forces that distort or constrain professional" (Yip, 2006, p. 246). Interestingly, referencing the "political conditions" in the above excerpt, and reflecting on how and why political ideology is manifesting in their consciousness, will provide social workers with keener insight into this phenomenon—and what to do about it. Yip (2006) articulates guidance in three stages of practical reflectivity based on prior authors' scholarship.

> Schon . . . described three levels of reflectivity: knowing in action, reflection in action and reflection on reflection in action. Reflection can be deeper and deeper, starting from being aware of one's performance and continuing to critically assessing one's ideology and beliefs behind one's thinking and feeling in the action. . . . Finally, the professional reaches a stage of critical reflectivity in his or her practice.

■ 129 ■

POLITICAL IDEOLOGY AND SOCIAL WORK PRACTICE

S/he is critical about his or her own feeling and attitudes (psychic reflectivity), conceptual underpinning (conceptual reflectivity) and the systematic frame of his or her intervention (theoretical reflectivity). (pp. 246–247)

Social workers fully engaged in practical reflectivity can use this concept to assess the cognitive, affective, and behavioral components of their political ideology.

Moreover, when social workers examine their *use of self* (Arnd-Caddigan & Pozzuto, 2008), such practical reflectivity is supported. Practitioners can identify how all dimensions that comprise their work—their professional knowledge, their professional experience, their personality characteristics, and their commitment to clients—interplay with their political ideology. Effective practice requires the reflection of critiquing the use of self in client relationships (Arnd-Caddigan & Pozzuto, 2008). Social workers can examine how their self-identity, both as an individual person and as a social worker, impact and are impacted by such interplay. Use of self can integrate with the three stages of practical reflectivity as social workers can reflect using both their social work identity and their individual identity. In turn, all of these variables impact the therapeutic alliance. Table 5.2 provides questions to guide social workers in engaging in practical reflectivity and the use of self.

ENGAGEMENT IN ETHICAL DECISION MAKING

The value conflict grounded in political diversity may appear to be substantial. That an apparent ethical tension exists—between

POLITICAL IDEOLOGY AND SOCIAL WORK PRACTICE

TABLE 5.2 Examining Political Ideology in Practice through Practical Reflectivity and Use of Self

Psychic Reflectivity	Conceptual Reflectivity	Theoretical Reflectivity
What I am thinking about my client's presentation relating to their political ideology?	How did I formulate my political ideology on this particular policy?	How is any congruence of political ideology on a particular policy impacting my assessment and intervention in practice?
How I am feeling about my client's presentation relating to client's own political ideology?	How do I think the client formulated their political ideology on a particular policy?	How is any discordance of political ideology on a particular policy impacting my assessment and intervention in practice?

Source: Draws on Arnd-Caddigan (2009); Yip (2006).

social worker and client—is true. After all, social workers can have strong attitudes and emotions about different policy positions that can manifest in practice. Yet, when closely examining the tension with respect to what do about it, the answer may be easier to resolve than what appears on the surface. When the ethical principles of social justice and self-determination collide, self-determination should prevail. Why? Because social workers honor self-determination of clients, and aside from intervening when there is real or threatened harm to themselves

POLITICAL IDEOLOGY AND SOCIAL WORK PRACTICE

or others, self-determination is the route to follow. This means respecting self-determination of political ideology, although it gets complicated when the client pushes the social worker outside the realm of law.

We return to two of the earlier vignettes in which the social worker thinks the client is harming: 1) a client who is considering PAS as well as one who is not; and 2) a client who believes that her husband's paid work trumps her own work is okay to believe this. Outside the gentle role of educator and the deft skill of challenging a client's beliefs, a social worker ultimately respects the clients' self-determination. To the extent that it is challenging for social workers to do this suggests how individual social workers, and the profession as a whole, might need to further stretch themselves to truly accommodate different political beliefs.

We return now to the other two vignettes. These differ from the others as the unfairness of the system is potentially causing harm. Here, social justice might trump self-determination as the client might not be aware that social justice can be achieved. For example, for the client who earns $500 over the income eligibility for SNAP, we can easily see, from the left, that the capitalistic system is rigged and citizens should at least receive welfare benefits such as SNAP. The client isn't harming but rather the client is being harmed by an unfair system. Therefore, a social worker might believe that it is acceptable to encourage the client to not report certain tips so the client meets TANF's income eligibility.

In the other vignette, the social worker considers placing a young child with a potential guardian who is residing illegally in the United States. While the social worker might believe that the adult should be here legally, assuming a clearance and home visit are successful, ultimately, the client may best be served with this relative. In this case, the social worker's sense of social justice is substituted for the young child's self-determination. On the other hand, a social worker who is more conservative may believe that this relative should be understandably deported as the nation must support its laws. The social worker would strive to find another permanent options for the child.

Addressing the ethical issues of political ideology is demanding—and the degree of challenge hinges on whether the client is perceived to be harming or receiving harm that ultimately manifests in political ideology and its ethical tension. We can take guidance on decision making from Reamer (2006), who supports assessment of the tension, evaluating the impact on all stakeholders, consulting with experts and ethical codes and other resources, making a determination, and continuing to monitor and evaluate the outcome. Galambos (2009) concurs that "change occurs through movement toward a resolution of conflicts between students' personal values and social work values" (p. 346).

THE ROLE OF SUPERVISION

The use of supervision is central to effective professional development and practice (National Association of Social Workers, 2013). Social workers—new to the field and seasoned alike—can discuss their political countertransference in supervision and

POLITICAL IDEOLOGY AND SOCIAL WORK PRACTICE

identify the particular value or value conflict that is challenging them in their direct work. Furthermore, they can share their insights from practical reflectivity and use of self and work with their supervisor to reach enlightenment and resolution. Supervision has a profound effect on the social worker's professional development and practice (Shulman, 2008).

Questions that can be asked in supervision include the following:

1) Why is the social worker's political ideology relevant to the presenting issue?

2) What is the underlying value associated with this ideology?

3) What is the perceived value associated with the client's political ideology?

4) What is the value conflict?

5) How does this value conflict prevent effective work with the client?

Together, the supervisor and social worker can create a plan of action for the social worker's continued professional development and then continue to review this plan for feedback and growth. Using supervision is essential as a social worker cannot terminate a client and refer them to another social worker due to a perceived or real political ideological difference. While the NASW *Code of Ethics* (2021a) is clear in its charge that social workers should not operate outside of their realm of professional practice, they should work with a client regardless of differences in political ideology. A social worker also cannot pass over a client on a waiting list because the client's

■ 134 ■

POLITICAL IDEOLOGY AND SOCIAL WORK PRACTICE

political ideology (based on status or actual presenting issue) runs counter to their own.

For example, social workers who are more conservative or New Right in political ideology may wish to "refer out" a same-sex married couple, an undocumented immigrant, a woman who is adamant about having an abortion, or a terminally ill person who is invested in exploring PAS. Conversely, social workers who are more liberal or New Left may not want to take a client who is very pro-life, counsel a couple with traditional notions of gender and marriage, or work with a client who is adamant about not taking a government-mandated vaccine.

As tempting as it may be to avoid such cases, Timbers & Yancy (2021) remind readers that social workers must "take internal inventory of one's biases and assumptions to best assert or bracket out personal convictions from policy formation and implementation" (p. 134; see also Witt et al., 2022). While one can make the argument that referring out is ethical when social workers know that their bias is so deep rooted (Winter et al., 2015), this is often not pragmatic given fewer resources available. Therefore, supervision plays a pivotal role in helping the social worker grow in professional development to ensure that quality client care and sound practice occurs.

POLITICAL DIVERSITY AND AGENCY PRACTICE

Having reviewed political diversity and clinical practice, let's turn to several considerations of political ideology in mezzo practice.

MISSION CONGRUENCE AND AGENCY EMPLOYMENT

Political diversity can manifest at the organizational level, and one way this is demonstrated is through mission congruence (Rosenwald and Hyde, 2006). Organizational missions are central to agencies' work as they guide the organization's resources to some common good of client betterment (Kirst-Ashman & Hull, 2018). An agency's mission can actually be viewed through a political ideological frame. For example, what does the mission articulate about moral issues, civil rights issues, welfare eligibility issues, and even basic system commitments (Brint, 1994)? Do the agencies articulate in their mission any particular policy relevant to *Social Work Speaks* (National Association of Social Workers, 2021b)?

As examples, we examine mission statements from two agencies where social workers might find employment. Their names are familiar to us and see reproductive choice in different perspectives.

Here is the mission from Planned Parenthood (2021):

- Help people live full, healthy lives—no matter your income, insurance, gender identity, sexual orientation, race, or immigration status;
- Provide the high-quality inclusive and comprehensive sexual and reproductive health care services all people need and deserve—with respect and compassion;
- Advocate for public policies that protect and expand reproductive rights and access to a full range of sexual and reproductive health care services, including abortion;

POLITICAL IDEOLOGY AND SOCIAL WORK PRACTICE

- Provide medically accurate education that advances the understanding of human sexuality, healthy relationships, and body autonomy;
- Promote research and technology that enhances reproductive health care and access.

The mission from Catholic Charities of the Rio Grande Valley (2021) is supported by one of its guiding principles, "Life and Dignity of the Human Person":

> The Catholic Church proclaims that human life is sacred and that the dignity of the human person is the foundation of a moral vision for society. This belief is the foundation of all the principles of our social teaching. In our society, human life is under direct attack from abortion, euthanasia and the death penalty. We believe that every person is precious, that people are more important than things, and that the measure of every institution is whether it threatens or enhances the life and dignity of the human person.

Social Work Speaks (National Association of Social Workers, 2021b) advocates for women to have reproductive choice; therefore, social workers whose political ideologies aligned with *Roe v. Wade* will likely find working at Planned Parenthood much more fulfilling than Catholic Charities. The reverse is true for social workers who do not agree with NASW's (2021b) statement on reproductive choice; their convergent ideology on this policy probably would lead to them applying for employment at Catholic Charities. Regardless of political ideology on this particular topic, this dynamic would be one consideration in a social worker's employment and perhaps in the decision to stay at that organization. Likewise, human resource considerations aside, employers might need to judge the suitability of candidates or consider retaining a social worker whose views may not align with their mission statements.

RESOURCE ALLOCATION AND AGENCY REGULATION

It is good practice for social workers to advocate for resources given the bureaucratic structures in which agencies exist. After all, advocacy is fundamental to the social work profession (Hoefer, 2019). From this vantage point for organizational practice, advocacy is "action in a systematic and purposeful way to defend, represent, or otherwise advance the cause of one or more clients at the . . . organizational . . . level in order to promote social justice" (Hoefer, 2019, p. 3). Typically, such advocacy is part of the routinized processes at an agency. If a client needs assistance with an energy bill, perhaps the agency has funds. If a client needs assistance with a gift card for a supermarket, perhaps the agency has funds. Based on both stated procedures and effective advocacy, social workers can provide these important resources to assist their clients.

As mentioned, bureaucracy by nature is governed by, and at times, mired in regulations. These regulations are germane to our discussion when they are rooted in particular political ideologies that help—or hinder—the social worker's ability to

POLITICAL IDEOLOGY AND SOCIAL WORK PRACTICE

advocate effectively. Reamer (2005) informs us about the nature of these regulations:

> Social workers need to be aware of a wide range of federal, state, and local regulations. Regulations are legally enforceable guidelines promulgated by government agencies. For example, the federal government's Department of Health and Human Services, Department of Housing and Urban Development, and Department of Justice have implemented many regulations that are relevant to social work, such as regulations concerning eligibility for disability benefits, eviction from federally subsidized housing . . . and funding of services for people who are HIV positive or who have AIDS. Administrative agencies have the legal authority to enforce regulations once the sponsors have followed strict procedures to solicit public comment, conduct public hearings, and review the regulations for cost and consistency with other regulations and laws (the so-called Administrative Procedures Act). (p. 164)

The examples above reflect political ideological positions on "fairly" set benefit ceilings for those with disabilities, "fairness" for those who have been evicted, and "sufficiently" funded services for individuals living with HIV. At some point, regulations must be established regarding criteria to receive or lose a welfare benefit. Sufficient funding is always an essential factor as well. Those who think that these regulations are "fair" reflect a certain political ideology. Those who believe that guidelines are too strict and too limiting, or who are underfunded, would reflect a more moderate to conservative ideology. Those who believe, for example, that the federal government should provide free housing to all of its citizens would be operating from the New Left. These examples recall Rawls's (1971) important concept of the "right" amount of dividends for individuals—in terms of the nature, scope, quantity, and process. Additionally, these examples recall the chapter's earlier vignettes on the parameters of the law and political ideology.

As we consider the formula for creating social welfare benefits in the first place—and the eligibility standards by which such benefits are allocated, we can glimpse the political ideologies aligned with such calculations. For example, "desert" or deservingness is the resource allocation principle that people deserve something if they work hard for it (Barusch, 2018). This method honors a conservative ideology of first come, first served and the rugged individualism of the Protestant ethic. There are instances when diligence and hard work are cast aside—across the political spectrum—if human suffering is caused by natural or human disaster. In these cases, the sources of the individuals' plights are perceived as outside of their own responsibility; this is why there is broad bipartisan support for disaster and antiterrorism relief and intervention.

But for those individuals whose life circumstances stem from poverty, most substance abuse, and some mental illness, conservative social workers may believe their assistance should come from private charity, and government resources are not warranted; here the rugged individualism tenet of conservative and New Right ideology is prevalent. However, for liberal social

POLITICAL IDEOLOGY AND SOCIAL WORK PRACTICE

workers, poverty, substance abuse, and all mental illnesses are at least partially maintained by both unfair economic systems and treatment systems. Extending this liberal ideology is the notion of affirmative action in which historical trauma warrants targeted and systemic intervention (Rosenwald, Baird & Williams, 2023). In fact, a Progressive ideology suggests reparations are necessary for African Americans, for example, to more significantly address slavery-born inequities (Jones, McElderry & Conner, 2022).

CONCLUSION

This chapter explored the intersection of political diversity and practice. It further discussed the concept of political countertransference and provided an ethical framework—including conceptions of "harm" that might guide political ideology formation. Social workers can address political countertransference, drawing on practical reflectivity and use of self, engaging in ethical decision making, and employing supervision in addressing any tensions that derive from conflicts of political ideology. Several considerations of political diversity's intersection with agencies are identified as well as an examination of how political ideology intersects with resource allocation. Understanding the variable of political diversity against this practice backdrop holds much promise.

Chapter Six

A MODEL FOR RECONCILING POLITICAL DIVERSITY AMONG SOCIAL WORKERS

A MODEL that more deeply addresses political diversity among social workers has been put forward. The focus on political ideology draws upon the social empathy framework (Segal, 2011; Segal & Wagaman, 2017) and expands on social responsibility in Segal's model based on assumption of free will and consequent moralization (Everett et al., 2021). This model embeds these ideas utilizing intergroup dialogues (Dessel & Rodenborg, 2017a) to promote and advance reconciliation between social workers' sense of self-determination and sense of social justice. This dialogue can be used in educational and postgraduate professional settings. Figure 6.1 presents this schematic.

SOCIAL EMPATHY FRAMEWORK

The social empathy framework (Segal, 2011) is a useful construct that focuses on the role of social empathy in achieving

A MODEL FOR RECONCILING POLITICAL DIVERSITY

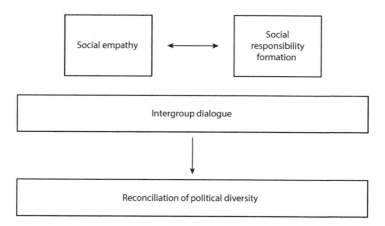

FIGURE 6.1 A model for reconciling political diversity among social workers.

social justice. The essential components are empathy, contextual understanding, and social responsibility (Segal, 2011).

> Social empathy applies empathy to social systems to better understand the experiences of different people, communities, and cultures. Social empathy is the combination of: 1) experiencing empathy to its fullest extent; 2) gaining deep insight and knowledge about historical and socioeconomic contexts, particularly in relation to inequality and disparity; and 3) embracing the importance of social responsibility. These experiences, knowledge, and beliefs combine to galvanize us to act in ways that promote social justice. Social empathy provides the pathway for creating communities and social policies governed by empathy. (Segal, 2011, pp. 267–268)

A MODEL FOR RECONCILING POLITICAL DIVERSITY

In their research, Segal and Wagaman (2017) argue that utilizing social empathy may ultimately override differences in partisanship and honor social work's mission to achieve economic and social justice. This is based on a three-tier model that builds social empathy through exposure, explanation, and experience (Segal, 2011). As participants, respectively, examine their differences, consider why differences occur, and situate themselves in each other's lives, "assess[ment should occur] as to whether empathy, contextual understanding, and social responsibility increase" (p. 275). The development of social responsibility is a valuable concept that is at the heart of political ideology (Abbott, 1988). A social empathy framework can incorporate a granular understanding of the construction of one's views on social responsibility in the formation of political ideology.

SOCIAL RESPONSIBILITY

The extent that an individual's problem is deemed a social problem determines assignment of blame and location of solution (i.e., within the individual, within government). Everett et al. (2021) learned that social responsibility is based on individuals' beliefs in the degree of "free will" and the consequent "moralization" or "assignment of blame" for the plight in which people find themselves. The authors argue that those with a more conservative political ideology are more likely to believe individuals have free will, and so when they suffer, such as in the case of unemployment or addiction, the individuals are responsible for

A MODEL FOR RECONCILING POLITICAL DIVERSITY

their own situation (Everett et al., 2021). Therefore, ascertaining social responsibility

> demonstrates that belief in free will is linked to a desire to hold people accountable for their moral wrongdoing, and that free will attributions vary as a function of the valence of the action, how moral or immoral it is perceived to be, and even who the target is. . . . For example, as illegal drug use is perceived to be more morally wrong, so too are drug users seen as more responsible and in control of their situation; and as being unemployed and receiving social welfare [from government] is seen to be more morally wrong, so too are people in such situations seen as being more responsible for and in control of their lot. The reason that political debates concerning responsibility and deservingness have been an enduring feature of political discourse throughout history is likely to stem, at least in part, from the powerful and often conflicting moral intuitions driving such judgments. (Everett et al., 2021, p. 480)

In sum, moral assumptions underpin political ideologies regarding assumptions of why people are in the predicaments they are in as well as the idea of self-determination. The idea of "blaming the victim" reflects a more conservative view when it comes to able-bodied individuals who are "responsible" for their predicament. "Blaming the system" encapsulates an essential conviction of a more progressive ideology. This deeper understanding of what constitutes social responsibility provides additional detail for the social empathy framework (Segal, 2011). This integrated knowledge describes how individuals form their

• 145 •

INTERGROUP DIALOGUES TO ADDRESS POLITICAL DIVERSITY AMONG SOCIAL WORKERS

As referenced in chapter 4, intergroup dialogues (IGDs) are a valuable pedagogical tool to promote empathy and facilitate difficult conversations about members' experiences with societal oppression and privilege (Gurin, Nagda, & Zimena, 2013).

> IGD is a pedagogy designed to promote an understanding of social identity and social inequality to help students bridge segregation and begin to understand the life experiences of people perceived as different from themselves, to build relationships across differences, and to foster social justice. ... IGD is a multicultural and social justice education pedagogy that is built on intergroup contact theory . . . and involves at least two social identity groups with a history of conflict. Participants engage in a face-to-face, cofacilitated, and sustained group experience over the course of a semester. . . . In this way, IGD is designed to provide some of the contact conditions needed to reduce prejudice. (Dessel & Rodenborg, 2017a, p. 225)

The pedagogy uses a four-stage model of a closed-group dialogue process with a set number of sessions. The stages include ground rule creation and relationship building; social identity, privilege, and discrimination exploration; impact of privilege and

A MODEL FOR RECONCILING POLITICAL DIVERSITY

discrimination examination; and identification of next steps after initial dialogue (Rodenborg & Bosch, 2007). In IGDs, the facilitators match the participants with respect to a particular privilege or oppression (Gurin, Nagda, & Zimena, 2013). For example, an intergroup dialogue that examined gender identity would have a focused discussion between an equal number of transgender and cisgender social workers. The cofacilitators would include one who identifies as cisgender and one who identifies as transgender.

Though IGDs are traditionally focused on groups with respective histories of privilege and oppression that center on a certain social variable (e.g., race or sexual orientation), they can be useful in bringing together students with different political ideologies to have an honest and sustained dialogue on their differences and perhaps find common ground. While there has been some discussion that conservative social workers feel oppressed in social work (Hodge, 2011), the oppression and privilege referenced in IGDs typically trace their origins to narratives of privilege and oppression in the greater society. While privilege and oppression of political diversity in social work needs further examination, stereotypes linger in society about one's political ideology by groups who do not share it. The structure and process of IGDs lend themselves well to an engaged and sustained interaction on diversity of political ideology.

UTILIZING INTERGROUP DIALOGUES TO ADDRESS POLITICAL DIVERSITY AMONG SOCIAL WORKERS

Table 6.1 shows the stages of intergroup dialogues (Dessel & Rodenborg, 2017a) linked to the levels of building social empathy

TABLE 6.1 Intergroup Dialogues Utilizing Social Empathy and Social Responsibility

IGD Stage (Gurin, Nagda, & Zimena, 2013)	Building Social Empathy Levels (Segal, 2011)	Social Responsibility (Everett et al., 2021)
Stage 1 Ground Rules and Relationship Building	Exposure	Establish mutual rapport as precursor for discussing social responsibility
Stage 2 Social Identity, Privilege, and Oppression	Explanation	Share views on responsibility (society/individual) for people's plight. Share views on the role of free will in determining people's plight
Stage 3 Impact of Social Structure on Individuals and Groups	Experience	Challenge each other's views on individual responsibility for a person's plights and assignment of blame for plights
Stage 4 Next Steps in Creating a More Collaborative Community	Experience	Determine how to cocreate social work or broader spaces to increase empathy relating to social responsibility

A MODEL FOR RECONCILING POLITICAL DIVERSITY

(Segal, 2011) and a particular focus on examining social responsibility (Everett et al., 2021). The dialogues would last for a minimum of four, two-hour sessions. Both training and activities from the University of Michigan Institute on Intergroup Dialogue would be very useful (University of Michigan, 2022). Two social work facilitators, representing different political ideologies, would be trained to facilitate the dialogue.

FIRST STAGE

The first stage focuses on welcoming members to the intergroup dialogue, establishing ground rules, discussing the potential for the IGD, and identifying member goals (Gurin, Nagda, & Zimena, 2013). The Exposure level of the social empathy framework is introduced here as members "visit new places and people who are different from you" in the safety of the group (Segal, 2011, p. 275). Social workers and students can describe how they self-identify politically by political ideology (e.g., moderate, liberal, conservative) or political party affiliation (Independent, Republican, Democrat).

SECOND STAGE

The second stage emphasizes describing and sharing one's political ideology and any oppression or privilege participants have experienced in their lives (or witnessed in the lives of others) that have led to the formation of their political beliefs. Additionally, they share their beliefs on the causes of people's plights (e.g., unemployment, addiction, poverty, teen pregnancy), the role of

A MODEL FOR RECONCILING POLITICAL DIVERSITY

free will, and the extent to which individuals themselves, or the government (or a private charity), are responsible for helping them. The Explanation level of the framework poses the following questions to members: "Who is different from me? How are they different? How do we describe those differences?" (Segal, 2011, p. 275). Participants can complete a political ideology scale that will help them examine their identity further.

THIRD STAGE

The third stage focuses on a much deeper examination of oppression and privilege and the impact of societal power in influencing people's lives. This is the stage of the IGD in which members are most vulnerable. Members share, listen, and gently challenge each other's beliefs on why people find themselves in predicaments in their lives. The role of free will and assignment of blame continues to be explored and, at times, challenged. The Experience level of the framework continues as members address this situation: "Put yourself into the life of a person of a different class, sex, ability, age, sexual identity, race, or national origin. What would your life be like if you were different? What opportunities would you have or would you miss?" (Segal, 2011, p. 275). An additional question is "How does your understanding impact how you would identify politically? Does it change it or not from your current ideology—why or why not?" Additionally, participants can complete a "political autobiography" that will help them understand how their lives over time and across experiences formed their political beliefs and, consequently, their political ideologies.

■ 150 ■

A MODEL FOR RECONCILING POLITICAL DIVERSITY

FOURTH STAGE

The final stage focuses on identifying next steps to continue to transform social work classrooms and the profession itself into a more socially empathetic one. Having journeyed through some difficult discussions, participants can identify the ideal world they would like to experience. At this point, gratitude exists for sharing some very personal experiences and challenging participants' prejudices of why people are oppressed as well as why people are privileged. Members may have had prejudices begin to change—not just regarding a "progressive" or "conservative" perspective but at a deeper level, and began to more clearly understand the best way that vulnerable people in society can and should be helped.

This model can be used in social work classrooms, NASW professional development meetings, and social work conferences. In this era of the pandemic, IGDs can occur virtually as well as in person. Any array of political topics (e.g., vaccine mandates, income assistance, abortion, civil rights, voting rights) might be covered. Certainly, there is much nuance with political ideology formation, but this model can help further the dialogue and cultivate social empathy.

Chapter Seven

REVISITING THE LANDSCAPE
OF POLITICAL DIVERSITY
IN SOCIAL WORK

SOCIAL WORKER. Pro-life advocate. Democrat. Republican. Pro-amnesty on immigration. Pro-"traditional" marriage. Libertarian. Pro-capitalist. Progressive. Neo-liberal. Anti-capitalist. Born-again Christian. Atheist.

In the current swirl of hyper-charged political rhetoric, the profession is not immune and it needs a guide to navigate this charged environment. Local politics, state politics, federal politics, international politics, and civil society are emblematic of people who are strident, at times, unwilling to reflect, and willing to stay in corners of arrogance and self-righteousness. This permeates political rhetoric and debate—from the Progressive left to the New Right.

The people just referenced include our clients, our students, our interns, our colleagues, and even ourselves. This book examined the context for this discussion of political diversity in social

REVISITING THE LANDSCAPE OF POLITICAL DIVERSITY

work. It reviewed the profession's history in a political context. It looked at the research examining this subject. Then, it identified key practice and education issues that emerge when considering political diversity in social work.

This final chapter examines four tenets gleaned from current scholarship on political diversity, recommends future scholarship questions and research methods, and concludes the book.

TENETS OF POLITICAL IDEOLOGY IN SOCIAL WORK

The following four tenets anchor the discussion and debate about political diversity in social work. The proposed relationship between them is shown in figure 7.1 and presented in the text below.

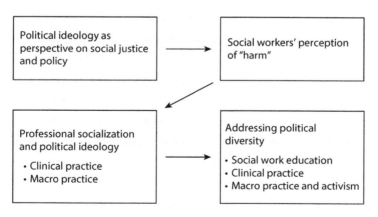

FIGURE 7.1 Tenets of political ideology in social work.

POLITICAL IDEOLOGY AS PERSPECTIVE
ON SOCIAL JUSTICE

Political ideology includes values on how society ought to be. Social workers espouse these values whether they are aware of them or not. Some champion their values and cite them as the very reasons they chose the profession. For these individuals, subscribing to these ideas (which are often liberal to very liberal, from the research) fuels their studies, their choice of employment, and their activism. For others, these values are held closely within and may—or may not—impact their social work practice.

Regardless of the degree of veil, political ideologies shape social workers' views on policy positions on social justice. As Rawls (1971) forwards, social justice seeks "to determine the appropriate distribution of the benefits and burdens of social life" (p. 51). Marginalized populations are burdened certainly with the inequities of social life; the values that social workers hold and the opinions that they form on the best policies that government can shape how they approach their clients in need (Rosenwald, Baird, & Williams, 2022). Achieving social justice reflects the best social system of policies to distribute limited resources of money, property, services, civil rights, and the like to populations marginalized by oppression (Barusch, 2018; Reisch, 2018). Yet it is essential to examine social workers' political ideologies as they impact ethical decision-making at all levels of practice (Reamer, 2013)

Indeed, social work practitioners and students bring an array of ideologies—more liberal though there are still some moderate and conservative ideologies—to their worldview of social

REVISITING THE LANDSCAPE OF POLITICAL DIVERSITY

justice. Supervisors in hospice care may be concerned a staff member who holds strong policy beliefs supporting a brain death may dishonor a client's living will. A social worker who disagrees with trans athletes competing in sports of their identified gender may unduly shape the client's decision to compete. A social work intern who believes capitalism is wrong may violate agency policy and provide an unallowable amount of supermarket gift cards to a client in need.

This dynamic is made more challenging because the profession interacts with clients who are members of privileged and marginalized groups, and the clients hold their own positions of political ideology and social justice and want to know if their social worker aligns with their own worldview. Clients engage with social workers with the clients' own vast range of ideas on how a social worker, or a social worker's supervisor or organization, or society itself should act. How social workers consider and respond to these engagements leads to a discussion of perceived harm.

SOCIAL WORKERS' PERCEPTION OF HARM

When some aspect of the social good is threatened, we can think that apparent harm is occurring or may be soon. As described in chapter 5, harm is an idea discussed by Rosenwald & Hyde (2006) to be a perceived affront to social justice. Underlying harm is the idea that some aspect of people's life quality is being threatened; referencing the social justice discussion, some resource of income, housing, civil rights, or program is not being provided in an adequate way to ensure life quality for one social group. This is the origin of privilege and oppression as certain groups are accorded benefits or face risks based on group membership.

Broadly, social workers may believe social policy should be more compassionate or more stringent. They may ideologically disagree with their clients, their colleagues, their supervisors, or the very organizations in which they intern or work. Some examples from Rosenwald's (2006b) study on political diversity of social workers are repeated from chapter 3 for participants' real examples of what can be perceived as harm to social justice:

- A very liberal participant said, "I dropped my membership last year. [NASW] needs to be a more radical [left] organization [and] inspire more activism among its members."
- A conservative participant stated NASW is "not an effective organization—politically liberal and advocates for the government to provide more and more—what about personal responsibility?"
- A moderate participant found "NASW's political agenda is much too liberal and has shifted away from the original mission to represent the poor and disenfranchised."
- A New Left participant said, "My beliefs, particularly around economic justice/the need for redistribution of wealth, 'narrowing the gap,' aren't addressed in the more radical manner I hold them."
- A conservative participant felt that "NASW is very liberal in its platform ideology (e.g., abortion, women's right to choose); my religious convictions are counter to the spirit

of NASW. . . . I don't believe any discrimination is right; however, I see homosexuality as a choice—which is a sin in God's eyes. NASW seems to validate a homosexual lifestyle as okay, one not to be discriminated against— I have a problem with this."

- A moderate participant stated, "We need diversity of opinions. I find it highly objectionable when the profession asserts, we should all be liberal thinkers!" (pp. 69–71)

Combatting harm or injustice by seeking social justice is routinely examined in social work education and practice (Barusch, 2018; Hoefer, 2019). After all, social justice is referenced in NASW's *Code of Ethics* (2021a) as one of the six central standards and undergirds *Social Work Speaks* (National Association of Social Workers, 2021b). Deciding on which resources of services, civil rights, vouchers, or tax credits should be distributed—and how they should be distributed equitably—is at heart of addressing this "harm to society." Yet that such a range of political ideologies exist makes it more complex for schools and departments of social work and organizations to determine this best mix. This leads to a discussion of the role of professional socialization in social workers' political ideology and social justice formation.

PROFESSIONAL SOCIALIZATION AND POLITICAL IDEOLOGY

Professional socialization is the purview of social work education and practice supervision. Faculty understand that student socialization is a process and that some prejudicial or disparaging comments students may make need to be processed. Faculty may also assume that there is a need to socialize students to a cause advocacy agenda for social justice. When encountering students with such a diverse range of political ideology, how do faculty consider the best approach to engage in a dialogue? Similarly, how do social work supervisors engage on this topic with their new employees in supervision?

The most important distinction is recognizing a conflation of political ideology may occur at both the micro and macro levels. In other words, a social worker has an individual political ideology that could impact clinical practice and this is distinct from the profession's political ideology that relates to cause advocacy efforts. Delineating this distinction is important.

POLITICAL IDEOLOGY AND CLINICAL PRACTICE

In preparation for and delivering clinical practice, there is no place for students or social workers to espouse prejudice based on any demographic variable. Faculty and supervisors should take this seriously and provide some professional socialization (particularly for students) through self-awareness, education, and dialogue. It is up for debate whether the faculty member or supervisor can eradicate the prejudice within the student or only help them not have it play out in their practice. Classrooms and supervision sessions should be safe spaces to explore even taboo topics such as prejudice. Helping students and new social workers check their political countertransference is useful so they can be aware of how their ideologies could impact practice.

REVISITING THE LANDSCAPE OF POLITICAL DIVERSITY

For example, a student who believes individuals who are LGBTQ should be "out and proud" needs to be made aware that they shouldn't foist this view on their clients. Conversely, an antivaccination social worker should feel comfortable exploring vaccine options with a client at the client's request.

Socialization in social work education and supervision with respect to political ideology means honoring students' and new social workers' self-determination to hold their views on social justice up to a point, and that is where the line is drawn. Are there expectations of which lines cannot be crossed for social worker degree seekers to call themselves a social worker? In Flaherty et al.'s (2013) study, the only characteristic that would ban a social worker from the profession is being racist.

POLITICAL IDEOLOGY AND MACRO PRACTICE

Conversely, the profession socializes students and social workers into its legislative agenda and advocacy efforts by simply asking everyone to support it. Each year, NASW—both the national office and the state chapters—develop legislative agendas that focus on support and modification to bills to promote social work policy positions and values. Local units (at the county level, for example) are welcome to develop legislative agendas as well.

The annual legislative agenda of the NASW Board of Directors must align with NASW's policy priorities and the policy statements from *Social Work Speaks* (National Association of Social Workers, 2021b). The NASW Delegate Assembly is charged every three years with formulating the policy statements of the profession and produces *Social Work Speaks*. This tome's importance cannot be understated. Referenced throughout this book, *Social Work Speaks* (National Association of Social Workers, 2021b) is the primary resource source for policy statements that represent what the profession believes is essential for clients and communities. It is the realization of the *Code of Ethics*'s call for social justice (National Association of Social Workers, 2021a). It contains dozens and dozens of policy statements that guide social workers and the profession at large as they engage in activism via lobbying efforts and policy briefs to the president of the United States among other political actors (including the Trump and Biden administrations (National Association of Social Workers, 2016; National Association of Social Workers, 2021c).

Inherent in these legislative agendas are political ideologies that respond to need, articulate the role of government, and propose the social welfare benefit (e.g., free community college, a tax credit, a civil right, or a vocational service) that should be provided by federal, state, or local government. The following text box provides NASW's 2021–2022 legislative agenda. Many of the policy statements in *Social Work Speaks*, as introduced in chapter 1, are realized in this agenda.[1]

The implications of socializing social workers into inherent political ideologies via a legislative agenda bear examination (Epstein, 2011). As mentioned, NASW serves as the proxy for the profession's official voice—defaulting to the formal voice of the organization due to its longevity, largest social work membership, and organizational structure. It is worth noting that

NASW 2021–2022 POLICY PRIORITIES (LEGISLATIVE AGENDA) FOR THE BIDEN-HARRIS ADMINISTRATION

Support Our Essential Social Work Workforce

The nation's 700,000 social workers are an essential workforce and have been since the founding of the profession over a century ago. We are among the most racially diverse mental and behavioral health and health-care professions and provide critically needed services to millions of Americans every day in a broad range of settings including health-care facilities, schools, child welfare, community agencies, correctional institutions, and private practice.

Continue COVID-19 Recovery

NASW looks to the Biden-Harris administration and Congress to galvanize the country around fighting the country's most devastating public health crisis since 1918, and its many impacts. The rapid deployment of the COVID-19 vaccines is crucial in our recovery, and the relief packages to date continue to be instrumental in mitigating the devastation. But more action is needed to save lives and livelihoods.

(continued on next page)

(continued from previous page)

Improve Access to Mental and Behavioral Health and Social Care Services

Mental and behavioral health are crucial components of overall health. Social workers play a crucial role in promoting mental and behavioral health and do so in a broad range of settings and communities and with a wide array of populations.

Provide High-Quality Health Care for All

NASW supports the enactment of a national health-care policy that ensures access to a full, coordinated continuum of physical, mental health, and social care services for all people. A single-payer system that ensures universal access to these services is the best means to achieve this goal, and the Affordable Care Act moves the nation in the right direction.

Build Healthy Relationships to End Violence

Interpersonal violence has a traumatizing impact across the life span on individuals, families, communities, and society. Developing and broadly implementing interventions to promote healthy relationships and reduce violence should be a high priority for policy action.

Advance Long and Productive Lives

By working together, the social work profession, NASW, and the federal government can create a society in which older adults and people of all ages thrive.

Eradicate Social Isolation

Social isolation is a silent killer—as dangerous to health as smoking. Our challenge is to educate the public on this dual health hazard, support health and human service professionals in addressing loneliness and social isolation, and promote policies that deepen social connections and community for people of all ages.

End Homelessness

Our nation may be facing the most severe housing crisis in its history. In the absence of robust and swift intervention, an estimated 30 to 40 million people in America could be at risk of eviction in the next several months.

Create Social Responses to Climate Change

Climate change is one of the greatest threats to human health, mental health, and societal well-being that the world has ever faced.

(continued on next page)

(continued from previous page)

The health and mental health impacts of climate change and climate pollution also damage our economy. The toll on our health and economy continues to rise as we delay action.

Harness Technology for Social Good

New technologies can be deployed in order to more strategically target social spending, speed up the development of effective programs and interventions, and bring a wider array of help to more individuals and communities.

Eliminate Racism

Corrective action is essential to abate long-standing inequities associated with systemic discriminatory practices. Our leaders (with support of the general public) must transform their understanding of the system of oppression and the factors that keep it in place and take actions that make our society more equitable and inclusive for all people.

Build Financial Capability for All

We can reduce economic hardship and the debilitating effects of poverty by adopting policies that bolster lifelong income generation and safe retirement accounts; expand workforce training and retraining; and provide financial education and access to high-quality and efficient financial services.

Reduce Extreme Economic Inequality

A persistent cycle of economic insecurity has ensnared working Americans for decades as they encounter the unpredictable events of social life and the economic risk inherent in our economy. NASW calls on national leaders to implement a multifaceted approach to tackling poverty and creating economic stability.

Achieve Equal Opportunity and Justice

Addressing racial and social injustices, deconstructing stereotypes, dismantling inequality, exposing unfair practices, and accepting the super diversity of the population will advance this challenge. All of these actions are critical to fostering a successful society.

Advance Political Justice

The current lower federal court judges are young and highly ideological and do not reflect the modern United States.

Reform Immigration Policy

Nearly 1,000 policies attacking immigrants were issued by the prior administration. These xenophobic policies are antithetical to the principles of our Constitution and must be rescinded.

(continued on next page)

(continued from previous page)

Protect and Provide for Maltreated Children

It is essential that children who experience trauma as a result of child abuse, neglect, and other acts of violence receive proper support and services.

Serve America's Veterans and Their Families

A once declining veteran population is now increasing again and is in additional need of mental health treatment to address issues such as post-traumatic stress disorder, traumatic brain injury, depression, substance use disorder, domestic violence, and suicide.

Advance LGBTQ Rights

LGBTQ people do not have full civil and statutory protection under the law as defined in Title VII of the Civil Rights Act of 1964. Discrimination remains a widespread threat to LGBTQ people's well-being, health, and economic security.

Promote the Rights of People with Disabilities

Although there has been tremendous progress over the past few decades to address issues of disability rights violations, due in large part to enactment of the Americans with Disabilities Act, this community still experiences barriers, discrimination, and a lack of access to the full benefits of society.

Source: National Association of Social Workers, *Blueprint of Federal Social Policy Priorities* (2021c).

REVISITING THE LANDSCAPE OF POLITICAL DIVERSITY

other professional proxies exist, such as the National Association of Black Social Workers, Latino Social Workers Organization, and the North American Association of Christians in Social Work. Their collective voices, for our purposes through their legislative agendas, may support, counter, or most likely fluctuate with NASW's policies and, consequently, the profession's official political ideology. This is an important point, as which professional organization counts as the standard bearer? It is understandable why NASW takes the lead, but this assumption needs to be articulated from a standpoint of ideological inclusivity and professional socialization.

ADDRESSING POLITICAL DIVERSITY

We have examined political ideology in social work as a statement on social justice and that social justice underscores that any social harm occurring needs to be addressed. Both clinical and macro practice rely on socialization for students and social workers to prepare them for practice with a given political ideology.

But as we have seen, this plan is oversimplified. There is an inherent tension between the liberal ideology assumed of the profession and the diverse political ideologies that exist—from the left and from the center and right. This tension is indicated on perceptions of and solutions to harm or social injustice. What happens when professional socialization does not succeed or is incomplete; that is, what if social work students are only somewhat socialized into the expected political ideology?

REVISITING THE LANDSCAPE OF POLITICAL DIVERSITY

Does it matter more if this incomplete socialization occurs in clinical practice than complete subscription to the legislative agenda? Responding to this tension from an educator, clinical supervisor, and professional perspective is key, and these are reflected in addressing diversity in political ideology.

SOCIAL WORK EDUCATION

From chapter 4, a number of strategies were forwarded to facilitate the discussion of political diversity in the classroom. They are found in the following text box. Social work educators are encouraged to follow these strategies in both classwork and in the field with respect to pedagogy and assignments that honor both an explicit and implicit curriculum.

STRATEGIES TO ADDRESS POLITICAL DIVERSITY IN EDUCATION

1. Increase Instructor Awareness of Political Ideology Expression
2. Ensure Room for a Range of Political Ideology Expressions in the Classroom
3. Manage the Classroom Effectively
4. Employ Practical Reflectivity
5. Implement Intergroup Dialogue
6. Teach and Apply Ethical Decision Making

REVISITING THE LANDSCAPE OF POLITICAL DIVERSITY

A good start is for the professor and field educator to reflect on their own political countertransference of where they expect students to be with respect to political ideology expression. Once they do this, educators can create space in the classroom and field supervision to have open and honest discussions about political ideology. In classroom and group supervision, managing these discussions in respectful ways is key to having robust discussions of some expressions of political ideology that can conflict with faculty as well as other students' political ideologies. Promoting a reflective environment allows genuine dialogue to occur. This dialogue can occur free-floating as well as within the formal parameters of an intergroup dialogue. (The framework for an intergroup dialogue on political diversity is articulated in Chapter 6.)

If an absolute expression of political ideology results in prejudice, this may be the litmus test in which the educator brings in the application of ethical decision making and asks students to weigh student self-determination versus social justice. In this era, clients who are undocumented, individuals who are transgender, and women who seek abortion services may be the most polarizing groups for some conservative students to work with. Conversely, working with clients who are racist, homophobic, antivaccine, or espouse conspiracy theories about the sanctity of elections may be difficult for a set of progressive students to work with. Of course, any student might have an issue with these clients. What all of these have in common is that a prejudice may exist that is connected to a social policy and political ideology. Educators should draw the line here and assert that students' self-determination about who they wish to work with only extends so far.

On the issue of prejudice, social justice should prevail, and students who are not comfortable working with certain groups of clients—based on an acknowledged or unacknowledged bias—should be referred to administration for appropriateness of fit with the profession. This may be social work education's only line in the sand when it comes to socialization into a political ideology expression. Of course, the *Code of Ethics* (National Association of Social Workers, 2021a) underscores that social workers should not demonstrate prejudice toward their clients, and this expectation corresponds with this expectation of socialization. Only without demonstrating prejudice or discrimination can social workers be deemed legitimate.

Indeed, Galambos (2009) believes that social work education can teach values while accounting for political diversity. She writes, "Planned teaching of professional social work values can influence the shaping of tolerance appropriate for social work practice while allowing for political diversity. If we believe that education can influence opinions, values, world views, and professional conduct, then implementing a true deliberative classroom environment can be a more effective method for embracing political tolerance. Viewing political tolerance as an acceptable value of democratic societies can lead to a better understanding of political diversity within" (p. 346). Practicing political tolerance while ensuring that lines of harmful prejudice are not crossed is the critical dynamic in the classroom.

CLINICAL PRACTICE

Similar to the previous discussion, there is even greater importance on the social worker who has left the student role and is employed, representing what a social worker is to the general population. The following text box summarizes strategies to facilitate political diversity expression developed in chapter 5.

STRATEGIES TO ADDRESS POLITICAL DIVERSITY IN CLINICAL PRACTICE

1. Identify Political Countertransference
2. Utilize Practical Reflectivity and Use of Self
3. Engage in Ethical Decision Making
4. The Role of Supervision

Identifying social workers' political countertransference is essential to help identify what in a client's political identity may be triggering to the social worker. For example, a social worker may believe vaccination mandates are essential in the pandemic response and, therefore, vaccine mandates are the realization of social justice regarding public health. Yet this expression of their ideology and a gentle effort to provide the client with vaccine education must be balanced with client self-determination. The social worker should not impose their view on the client.

This examination of political countertransference is made possible through reflectivity and the use of self in which the social worker is able to gain insight into the political ideology they exhibit and the potential conflict with a client's political ideology. While it is hoped that the social worker can engage in this reflectivity on their own, the role of supervision is crucial.

Supervision is central to social workers' onset of clinical practice as interns although the degree to which supervision continues—or exists—for social workers after postdegree internship and licensure varies. It is hoped that social workers who do not receive further directed supervision (e.g., those in private practice) still avail themselves of peer-supervision groups through NASW local units or other professional venues.

In supervision, a supervisor and social worker can develop a safe place in which the social worker can share honest views and potential conflicts that are rooted in political ideology. In supervision as well, ethical decision making applies to help the social worker examine the contours of the aforementioned self-determination–social justice dynamic. The social worker would examine if there is ever a situation in which a client's political ideology would make the social worker unable to assist. The answer should be an easy no. Social workers are educated to engage with all clients, whether they belong to social movements (e.g., Black Lives Matter) or espouse conspiracy theories (e.g., regarding the 2000 and 2020 U. S. presidential elections—from far left and far right camps, respectively) that conflict with the social worker's beliefs. Referring out should only occur due to social worker emergency or if the presenting client need is outside of scope of practice.

REVISITING THE LANDSCAPE OF POLITICAL DIVERSITY

In supervision, these strategies can extend to the comfort and political ideological fit of the social worker with their employing organization. Here, the conflict of political ideology is not of the political countertransference type regarding a client but a clash of the social worker's political ideology with the organization's policies (some organizational policies do represent a political ideology). For example, the progressive social worker may find it challenging to abide by an agency's policies to limit financial assistance. The conservative social worker may find the organization's policy to offer clients' birth control options counters their own political ideology on the issue. In these cases, the social worker would need to put aside their personal political ideology for their professional practice or possibly terminate their employment.

Finally, the supervisor should ensure the social worker is appropriately compartmentalizing their political ideology in practice (e.g., stridency for or against vaccine mandates or beliefs not supporting same-sex marriage). Supervision is absolutely essential to ensure to the degree possible that the social worker does not impose their political ideology relating to policy positions and, most importantly, where any negative prejudice may be exhibited. To this last point, once a social work student graduates into serving as a social worker, the window for evolution of prejudice reduction has closed. Students may get a pass and be asked to do a self-awareness assignment, but a social worker may be fired. Absent supervision, in the case of a social worker in private practice who does not have a supervisor, clients can report any concern to state regulatory agencies that govern social work licensure. There, clients who believe they

REVISITING THE LANDSCAPE OF POLITICAL DIVERSITY

were recipients of social work malpractice can complete a grievance procedure against their social workers, who the clients allege were prejudiced (or discriminated against them). This avenue of recourse's importance is noteworthy as this prejudice can be rooted in political ideology.

MACRO PRACTICE AND ACTIVISM

When discussing social workers' political ideology regarding the profession's views on social justice as a whole, should not the self-determination extended to clients to safeguard them from social workers be extended to social workers themselves? In other words, within the macro frame of political ideology housed in the profession's legislative agenda, both students and social workers should be accorded self-determination to form their own political ideologies—even if they are not fully aligned with NASW's policy priorities. This point suggests that socialization into the legislative agenda has its limits as well. Students and social workers will end up, through insight or original conviction, with a formation of political ideologies that vary in alignment with NASW. Consider the progressive social worker who supports President Biden's Build Back Better program and believes that the NASW is selling out in its support of a pared-down version. Here, this social worker may agree on the goal that NASW has but not on tactics—such as the pace of change regarding radical versus incremental change.

Legislative agendas are shaped by stakeholder needs in a given time and place and form the bedrock of lobbying efforts. NASW takes the lead in mobilizing social work students and social workers to effective advocate for this agenda with their elected officials. There is no political ideology litmus test for membership on the NASW's national board and chapters' boards of directors. Nor is there such a test for the myriad of social work students and social workers who advocate on issues relating to poverty, addiction, and undocumented immigrants' civil rights as part of advancing social work's (NASW's) legislative agenda (National Association of Social Workers, 2021c). Yet the liberal lean of the profession based on NASW's legislative agendas is still aligned most with the Democratic Party; this alignment between legislative agendas, and *Social Work Speaks* and NASW's policy priorities, champions the liberal political ideology emphasis over other politically aligned groups.

This conclusion is based, from chapter 1, on the congruence of NASW's national agenda with the Democratic Party platform. Now, the Democratic Party is a "big tent" that represents sizable progressive and liberal membership along with some center-left (liberal-moderate) members, yet liberal political ideology still dominates NASW's national agenda, which is born from its policy priorities and *Social Work Speaks* (National Association of Social Workers, 2021b).

The liberal nature of the legislative agenda may catalyze social workers' activism. Interestingly, the research finds social work students with the most liberal ideologies are most inclined to be activists (Mizrahi & Dodd, 2013; Dodd & Mizrahi, 2017; Fisher et al., 2001). It is reasonable that when social work educators teach about social policy and activism through organizing that they would utilize NASW's legislative agendas. Yet social work educators should be mindful of this bias, as mentioned

■ 175 ■

REVISITING THE LANDSCAPE OF POLITICAL DIVERSITY

in earlier sections. While legislative agendas may appeal to the most liberal students and catalyze their organizing, there may be moderate and conservative students—and yes, even some progressive students—who are not as inclined to agree with all of the agenda and, therefore, could have their activism thwarted.

Social work educators should be mindful, ever checking political countertransference, that when teaching about social justice and organizing that NASW policies may be starting out points instead of the final word. True, if legislative agendas are thought of as "living documents"—in fact, they are modified over time—then any disagreement on policy or strategy. from the left or the right can at least be acknowledged.

Similarly, this discussion on proving a space for agreement and disagreement to occur can happen within professional organizations, such as NASW state or international chapters and local units. For example,

Specifically, the NASW chapter could sponsor a forum on political ideology that explicitly addresses the relationship between social workers' political ideology and their perceptions of how different policies and laws should be. . . . Although immediate implications are confined to the particular state of focus, this study provides food for thought on what implications might occur for NASW and the profession at large. A national forum on political ideology . . . might be useful to explicate the debate that occurs every three years within the Delegate Assembly as *Social Work Speaks* policy statements are established and modified. The creation of such a forum honors the spirit of the respect for

REVISITING THE LANDSCAPE OF POLITICAL DIVERSITY

diversity of colleagues' political belief in the NASW Code of Ethics . . . and might result in moving beyond superficial sound bites of the "other" to greater understanding of those along the political spectrum without fear of instant dismissal or reprisal. (Rosenwald, 2006b, pp. 74–75)

Therefore, legislative agendas are the profession's best efforts to guide policy change toward social justice; however, the conversation needs to be clear that it is acceptable to dissent from portions of NASW's agenda from the left and the right.

A SCHOLARSHIP AGENDA FOR POLITICAL DIVERSITY IN SOCIAL WORK

We now turn to a scholarship agenda for political diversity in social work. Building on the past conceptual and empirical work, future questions to examine both theoretically and in research are considered.

CONCEPTUAL DIMENSIONS

The biggest questions in any professional inquiry fall under paradigm formulation and shifts (Kuhn, 1996). The social work field remains wide open to examine this "diversity" variable of political diversity. Defining what political diversity is, and that it is a legitimate variable worthwhile of continuing study, is a good beginning.

DEFINING POLITICAL DIVERSITY

Fortunately, growing literature has established political diversity—defined as diversity of political ideology—as a variable worthwhile of inquiry and application (Rosenwald, 2006a; Galambos, 2009; Flaherty et al., 2013, Ringstad, 2014). Political diversity has been conceptualized by self-identification of political ideology philosophy, alignment with the profession's policy statements (Abbott, 1988), and alignment with policies or policy statements external to the profession (Flaherty et al., 2013; Ostrander et al., 2017). These ingredients or conceptions of political ideology consider individuals' perception of society's goals (well-being vs. power) (Meindl, Iyer, & Graham, 2019), social empathy (Segal 2011), social responsibility, free will and assignment of blame (Everett et al., 2021), equality-related issues and basic system commitments, welfare state issues, civil liberties, civil rights issues, morality and military force issues (Brint, 1994), and Abbott's (1988) original work on basic rights, social responsibility, self-determination, and individual freedom.

Therefore, underlying self-described traditional notions of political ideology are even more foundational values (e.g., beliefs relating to individual freedom, free will, and power) that provide the bedrock for thinking about political ideology. These ideas are presented in table 7.1.

Future scholarship that wishes to address the diversity of political ideologies of social workers would benefit from more focus on the political ideologies' foundational dimensions in addition to the more "surface" concepts of identification of

REVISITING THE LANDSCAPE OF POLITICAL DIVERSITY

TABLE 7.1 Traditional Concepts of Political Ideology and Dimensions of Political Ideology to Explore

Traditional Concepts of Political Ideology	Dimensions of Political Ideology to Explore
• Self-identification of political ideology philosophy	1. Social Empathy
	2. Society's Purpose
• Alignment with the profession's policy statements	3. Free Will
	4. Social Responsibility
• Alignment with policy statements external to the profession	5. Morality and Military Issues
	6. Basic Rights
• Political party affiliation	7. Individual Freedom
	8. Self-Determination
	9. Economics
	10. Civil Rights

Source: Draws on Abbott (1988), Brint (1994), Everett et al. (2021), Meindl, Iyer, & Graham (2019), and Segal (2011)

self-ranked ideology and alignment with a political party affiliation and particular policy. In other words, more depth of knowledge and understanding would be gained by understanding social workers' beliefs about social empathy, society's purpose, free will, and the like.

POLITICAL DIVERSITY AND PRIVILEGE AND OPPRESSION IN SOCIAL WORK

Diversity variables tend to have a privilege and oppression history grounded in larger society; for political diversity in social work, this may look a little different. Oppression has been cited

REVISITING THE LANDSCAPE OF POLITICAL DIVERSITY

as more applicable to more conservative practitioners in social work when they are students (Hodge, 2014; Will, 2007). But the notions of privilege and oppression based on political ideology have not been fully explored in social work—either in social work education or, particularly, in social work practice. For example, while oppression toward conservative social work students has been evidenced, at times, conceptual work has not explored oppression for progressive students regarding their ideologies and how evident they experiences are. Therefore, fully exploring privilege and oppression among the full spectrum of political ideology in both social work education and in social work practice bears examination. This exploration can be supplemented by focusing on predictors of ideology, including age, race, and religion.

EDUCATION IMPACT

The most conceptual examination has occurred with political ideology in social work classrooms. Examining how educators address political diversity in the classroom can be strengthened with a review of the creation of safe spaces to address political diversity (Flaherty et al., 2013). We can also examine how political ideology is addressed in field placements. The role of education in socialization into values bears further review, especially considering when socialization does not produce expected social work values. "In social work, like all professions, it is generally expected that students will be socialized to the articulated core social work goals and values when they receive their MSW" (Mizrahi & Dodd, 2013, p. 581). What are the experiences of

REVISITING THE LANDSCAPE OF POLITICAL DIVERSITY

students when their goals/routes toward social justice vary outside the norm?

Furthermore, Rodenborg & Boisen (2013) argue that social workers' liberal ideology may still allow for "aversive" or covert racism; therefore, to reduce prejudice, pedagogical work that draws on aversive racism theory and intergroup contact and is linked to social justice interventions is needed. Research on addressing prejudice in social work education as it relates to political ideology formation and socialization would be useful.

PRACTICE IMPACT

The impact of political ideology on practice still needs further study. The focus on students' political ideology in field placements as well as all dimensions of clinical practice, organizational practice, and macro practice, such as legislative agenda setting, activism and community organizing, and electoral politics should be explored. While there is some examination and correlation of student activism and liberal political ideology (Mizrahi & Dodd, 2013; Dodd & Mizrahi, 2017), the examination of activism among practicing social workers was not found. Additionally, an exploration of type of practice setting (public, private for-profit, or private nonprofit) should occur as well. Finally, the role of and addressing of political ideology in the social work supervisory relationship has not been examined.

Interestingly, when we review the profession's history, the critique of the professionalization movement begun by allegiance to Freud resulted in an analysis that the profession slowed down or

REVISITING THE LANDSCAPE OF POLITICAL DIVERSITY

halted its liberal activism. A historical examination should occur on assessing apolitical trends in social work practice (including the current focus on neuroscience) and if these trends divorced social workers from their activist roots; this may reflect a de facto moderate to conservative ideology based on the lack of activism and, therefore, preservation of the status quo. This is in the context of Epstein (2011), who challenges us to review the "liberal mythology" of the profession. The impact of social workers' political ideology alignment with the profession's ideology can benefit from additional review (Rosenwald, 2006b).

EMPIRICAL DIMENSIONS

METHODS

Methodologically, the research collected has been largely quantitative There is opportunity for particular work in developing qualitative methodology as well as continuing the pursuit of quantitative studies.

SAMPLING STRATEGY

The majority of studies have engaged students as participants in classroom settings. As mentioned, there is little research on social work students in field placements or social workers in all practice settings. Moreover, the samples have focused on particular universities or a particular state. Much more research should examine multiple universities (religiously affiliated or

REVISITING THE LANDSCAPE OF POLITICAL DIVERSITY

historically Black universities) (Flaherty et al., 2013). We need to review national as well as international samples, and to the latter, examine how political ideology in social work may look different in other nations. Finally, random samples from multiple universities as well as purposive and snowball samples for qualitative studies should be employed.

MEASURES

Political ideology is a complex topic, so a single indicator may not fully capture what it is. It may be that political party affiliation is not the best indicator; too much diversity in policy views is currently housed within the Democratic and, increasingly, the Republican Parties. While continuing to study political party affiliation provides information, its usefulness may be limited. This is in light of the increasing number of individuals joining the No Party Affiliation (NPA) or Independent Party. When one subscribes to NPA, it is difficult to know to which policy views one subscribes.

Both self-ranked political ideology, generally on the liberal-conservative continuum and some version of Abbott's (1988) Professional Opinion Scale version, based on *Social Work Speaks* (National Association of Social Workers, 2021b), have been used the most in the social work literature. Abbott's scale was based on individual freedom, basic rights, social responsibility, and self-determination; perhaps even larger measures could be developed that have expanded versions of social responsibility, for example. Instruments from political science and political psychology can be utilized. Finally, on Abbott's (1988) renowned

■ 183 ■

scale, more than thirty years have passed, and the policy statements on which it was based have changed to a degree (ten editions of *Social Work Speaks* have been published). It is time to update Abbott's scale beyond a particular study and test its psychometric properties continuing to use factor analysis.

As discussed, the literature on political diversity is young. There is a need to pursue scholarship in a number of areas germane to the profession in social work education, practice, policy development, and professional socialization. Scholarship including both conceptual inquiry and empirical research questions are needed to guide the next steps in this field of inquiry. There is interplay between the two as conceptual development facilitates hypothesis testing and interview guide formulation, while findings from empirical research influence further thinking.

CONCLUSION

When reflecting on the political sociology of the social work profession, the evolution of social work since its inception showcases a profession that has oscillated based on the political ideological paradigms it has embraced. During the founding of the profession, both liberalizing and conservatizing forces were at work. In major social welfare policy eras such as The New Deal, Great Society, health-care reform, and the Patient Protection and Affordable Care Act and Build Back Better, the National Association of Social Workers (2021c) and its precursors espoused liberal political ideology. Flaherty et al. (2013)

identify that "social work is not a politically neutral profession. The essence of the profession . . . including the goal of achieving social justice for vulnerable groups, cannot be accomplished without a workforce that subscribes to these professional values themselves. It, therefore, is not surprising that the social work profession has historically attracted those who hold more progressive (or liberal) views toward many polarizing social issues such as abortion" (p. 60).

Yet the profession's support for capitalism distinguishes progressive from liberal ideology and, in fact, may more realistically represent an overarching liberal to moderate ideology. Reisch & Jani (2012) reference this when characterizing the profession representing neoliberalism, or a "liberal, modernist" paradigm that suggests support for capitalism. Elaborating, Reisch & Rohde (2000) critique the profession's purported progressive stance by claiming social justice is at the forefront "while its practice largely focuses on accommodation" (p. 1134). "Instead of challenging the premises, parameters and priorities of this system, social workers focus on channelling clients' needs and interventions within it. The unintended social control function this produces is masked by the rhetoric of social justice" (Reisch & Rohde, 2000, pp. 1134–1135). This critique is what Epstein (2011), again, means by the "liberal mythology" of the profession.

At times, it seems the profession cannot win. The charged nature of political ideologies from its opponents is articulated by Mizrahi & Dodd (2013), who write "On the conservative end, social work is attacked for being too activist and biased . . . [while] [o]n the liberal end, social work is criticized for not practicing what it preaches, that is, for not promoting a stronger activist, value-based profession committed to social justice and proactively working to reform social policy (p. 581). This critique suggests that the profession needs to recharge to address injustices and overcome its "complicity in historical injustices, often affecting poor people and families of color" (Deepak, Rountree, & Scott, 2015, pp. 107–108).

This complexity at the profession's policy level is somewhat replicated at the "rank and file" level. Dodd and Mizrahi's (2017) review on political ideology of social workers found up to 75 percent of social workers identify as liberal across studies, but the percentage drops when a moderate or independent ideology is added, and about 10 percent of social workers are conservative. Therefore, it is not surprising when Rosenwald (2006b) wrote of social workers' perspectives of each other:

> It turns out that the stereotypes of social workers, as identified by Dolgoff & Feldstein (2003, p. 301), as " 'bleeding hearts,' radicals, captives of and apologists for 'the establishment,' organizers of the poor, and servers of the middle class" are held not only by the public but by social workers about each other. These stereotypes originate, in part, from the varied political ideologies held by social workers, as detailed in the data, and their conceptions of what a social worker should be. They also provide a foundation upon which social workers make judgments about themselves and one another regarding the degree of fit between political ideology and the profession . . . [Social workers] decide how explicitly supportive a climate for such diversity [they desire] to create." (Rosenwald, 2006b, p. 75)

REVISITING THE LANDSCAPE OF POLITICAL DIVERSITY

In the pursuit of social justice, the profession's appeal for progressive social workers (Mizrahi & Dodd, 2013; Fisher et al., 2001) may surprise these workers since the profession doesn't push the status quo as much as progressives may like. Conversely, conservative and New Right political ideologies are closeted in social work classrooms (Flaherty et al., 2013).

We can learn that political diversity indeed does exist, and aside from blatant and subtle prejudice that should be addressed (Dessel & Rodenborg, 2017b), we can learn to talk with each other and not past one another (Flaherty et al., 2013; Galambos, 2009; Hodge, 2011; Rosenwald & Hyde, 2006, Rosenwald et al., 2012; Segal & Wagaman, 2017). Whether it is ideologies associated with vaccine mandates or unemployment interventions, the expressions of political diversity should be allowed if social work does indeed claim to have a "big tent." It should. With a focus on inclusivity, the profession must include almost all voices. We can accept that students will graduate with social work degrees with a range of political diversity. They will have their own goals and routes toward social justice. They will hopefully utilize political countertransference once employed; their supervisors should do this as well.

The profession is strengthened when even a still-taboo topic such as political diversity is named, explored, and respectfully discussed. In an era where political discourse in civil society is anything but civil, social work can take the vanguard of civil discourse in promoting increased professional cohesion as well as client, community, and national well-being.

EPILOGUE

THE SPIRIT in which this book was written was to comprehensively define and examine a domain of social work that has received little attention. In doing so, both the political rhetoric and the substantive policy disagreements that appear on the national, state, and local stages clearly permeate the profession. But this book has an optimistic outlook, and we can take cues from current political and policy discourse that glimpses of unity can still occur.

At the federal level, bipartisan support in Congress—in conjunction with the president—can and does exist. In the Trump administration, there was strong bipartisan support for funding of opioid addiction prevention and treatment. In the Biden administration, gun control legislation—though seen as too little by some—was passed in Congress; this was the first significant bipartisan gun control legislation passed in decades. Congress is moving in a bipartisan matter to clarify the vice

EPILOGUE

president's role in election certification. There is strong bipartisan support for supporting Ukraine in its efforts to defeat Russia in its invasion.

At the state level, with the devastation that Hurricane Ian created in Florida and other southeastern states, President Biden and Florida Governor DeSantis put aside their differences in a joint tour of the most affected region. They did not have to do a joint tour but both agreed it was the right thing to do.

This is not to say the picture is rosy. It is not. But not everything is lost in the swirl of political divisiveness as the rhetoric suggests.

And we can take these lessons to the social work profession. While I have never observed conflict regarding political diversity to be at a dire level in the profession, it has never been fully examined and discussed. At the end of the day, while study after study supports the most common political ideology of social workers as "liberal," there are sizable progressive, moderate, and conservative moderate and conservative flanks in the profession.

The profession needs to explicitly accept that diversity of political ideologies exists—in the classroom and in all levels of practice. What is important is to accept that this diversity occurs, provide developmental guidance to students and new social workers in supervision, and make sure the social workers can check their political biases at the office door. When it comes to legislative agenda setting and community organizing, the profession should be informed and led by the social justice that is articulated in NASW's *Social Work Speaks*.

We will rarely receive unanimity among social workers on any particular issue—either a policy goal or the means to attain it.

EPILOGUE

But we can have dialogues—facilitated by social work faculty and NASW state chapters and local units—to listen to each other, to respect each other, and to determine the right path forward. As long as this path is anchored in *Social Work Speaks* and NASW's *Code of Ethics*, and as long as we are able to acknowledge and respectfully disagree when appropriate, we will march toward progress and equity for our clients and build a stronger profession of social work.

APPENDIX

SAMPLE SYLLABUS ON POLITICAL DIVERSITY AND SOCIAL WORK

POLITICAL DIVERSITY AND SOCIAL WORK[1]

COURSE DESCRIPTION

This course examines the role of political diversity—that is, the array of political ideologies that manifest in the social work profession. As a newer diversity variable to consider in social work, attention is given to an overview of political diversity, its history in policy context, the state of its scholarship, implications for social work education and practice, and new frontiers in this focus area.

LEARNING OUTCOMES

a. Examine the definitions and scope of political diversity in social work.
b. Synthesize the history of the profession's political ideology in the profession's evolution.

APPENDIX

c. Articulate the profession's political ideology in shaping and responding to social welfare policy.
d. Assess the scholarship on political diversity and social work.
e. Critique the implications of political diversity and social work education.
f. Critique the implications of political diversity and social work practice.
g. Examine the new frontiers for political diversity and the social work profession.

UNITS AND READINGS

Unit 1: Overview of Political Diversity and Social Work

This unit examines the definition and scope of political diversity in social work. It invites students to review and critique political diversity as a diversity variable and examines the discourse on political diversity in the profession.

READINGS: TEXT AND ARTICLES

Rosenwald, M. (2023). Chapter 1 in *Political ideology and social work*. Columbia University Press.

Baradat, L. P., & Phillips, J.A. (2020). *Political ideologies: Their origins and impact* (11th ed.). Longman.

Brint, S. (1994). *In an age of experts: The changing role of professionals in politics and public life*. Princeton University Press.

National Association of Social Workers. (2021a). *Code of Ethics*. National Association of Social Workers. Retrieved from https://www.socialworkers.org/About/Ethics/Code-of-Ethics/Code-of-Ethics-English

■ 194 ■

APPENDIX

National Association of Social Workers. (2021b). *Social Work Speaks: NASW policy statements 2021–2023.* (2021) (12th ed.). National Association of Social Workers.

Rawls, J. (1971). *A theory of justice.* Harvard University Press.

Rosenwald, M. (2006a). Exploring the political ideologies of licensed social workers. *Social Work Research, 30*(2), 121–126.

Will, G. F. (October 14, 2007). Code of coercion. *The Washington Post.*

Unit 2: Political Ideology and Social Work in Historical Context

This unit reviews social work's history in the context of political diversity. The unit examines and critiques social work's linkage with social welfare policy development in the major U.S. presidential administrations since the profession's inception.

READINGS: TEXTS AND ARTICLES

Rosenwald, M. (2023). Chapter 2 in *Political ideology and social work.* Columbia University Press.

Abramovitz, M. (1998). Social work and social reform: An arena of struggle. *Social Work, 43*(6), 512–526.

Barusch, A. S. (2018). *Foundations of social policy.* Cengage.

National Association of Social Workers (2016). *NASW Statement on Donald J. Trump Election as 45th U.S. President.* National Association of Social Workers. Retrieved from https://www.socialworkers.org/News/News-Releases /ID/88/%22

National Association of Social Workers. (2019). *Social Work Reinvestment Act.* National Association of Social Workers. Retrieved from https://www .socialworkers.org/Advocacy/Policy-Issues/Social-Work-Reinvestment -Act

National Association of Social Workers. (2021c). *2021 Blueprint of Federal Social Policy Priorities.* National Association of Social Workers. Retrieved from https://www.socialworkers.org/Advocacy/Policy-Issues/2021-Blueprint -of-Federal-Social-Policy-Priorities

APPENDIX

National Association of Social Workers (2021d). *Interactive timeline*. National Association of Social Workers. Retrieved from https://www.socialworkers.org/news/facts/interactive-timeline-of-social-work-and-nasw

National Association of Social Workers. (2021e). *NASW calls for President Trump to be removed from office*. National Association of Social Workers. Retrieved from https://www.socialworkers.org/News/News-Releases/ID/2271/NASW-calls-for-President-Trump-to-be-removed-from-office

Reisch, M. (2018). *Social policy and social justice* (3rd ed.). Cognella.

Trattner, W. I. (1999). *From poor law to welfare state* (6th ed.) Free Press.

Virginia Commonwealth University (2021). *Social Welfare History Project*. Virginia Commonwealth University. Retrieved from http://www.social welfarehistory.com/

Unit 3: The Scholarship on Political Diversity and Social Work

This unit reviews the evolution of scholarship on political diversity and social work. Research on both the foundation of political diversity and particular policy positions is showcased. Particular focus on contemporary scholarship examines studies involving social work students.

READINGS: TEXT AND ARTICLES

Rosenwald, M. (2023). Chapter 3 in *Political ideology and social work*. Columbia University Press.

Abbott, A. A. (1999). Measuring social work values: A cross-cultural challenge for global practice. *International Social Work, 42*(4), 455–470.

Begun, S., Kattari, S. K., McKay, K., Ramseyer Winter, V., & O'Neill, E. (2017). Exploring U.S. social work students' sexual attitudes and abortion viewpoints. *Journal of Sex Research, 54*(6), 752–763.

Chonody, J. M., Sultzman, V., & Hippie, J. (2020). Are social work students concerned about the environment? The role of personal beliefs. *Journal of Social Work Education, 56*(4), 809–824.

APPENDIX

Kennedy, S. C., & Tripodi, S. J. (2015). The death penalty attitudes of social work students: Current and future opportunities. *Journal of Forensic Social Work, 5*(1–3), 201–233.

Danforth, L., Hsu, H. T., & Miller, J. W. (2020). Color-blind racial attitudes among social work students: Exploration of individual and social network correlates. *Journal of Social Work Education, 56*(3), 412–427.

Davis, A. (2019). Historical knowledge of oppression and racial attitudes of social work students. *Journal of Social Work Education, 55*(1), 160–175.

Delavega, E., Kindle, P. A., Peterson, S., & Schwartz, C. (2017). The Blame Index: Exploring the change in social work students' perceptions of poverty. *Journal of Social Work Education, 53*(4), 664–675.

Epstein, I. (2011). Whence and whither research on political diversity? Toward turning up the volume on a more research-based conversation. *Journal of Social Work Education, 47*(1), 163–172.

Findley, P. A., Edelstein, O. E., Pruginin, I., Reznik, A., Milano, N., & Isralowitz, R. (2021). Attitudes and beliefs about medical cannabis among social work students: Cross-national comparison. *Complementary Therapies in Medicine, 58*, 102716. McPherson, J., Villarreal-Otálora, T., & Kobe, D. (2021). Injustice in their midst: Social work students' awareness of immigration-based discrimination in higher education. *Journal of Social Work Education, 57*(1), 55–69.

Ringstad, R. R. (2014). Political diversity among social work students. *Journal of Social Work Values and Ethics, 11*(2), 13–22.

Park, Y., Torres, M., Bhuyan, R., Ao, J., Graves, L., & Rundle, A. (2022). Social workers' perceptions of structural inequality and immigrant threat: Results from a national survey. *Journal of Social Work Education, 58*(3), 449–471.

Witt, H., Younes, M. K., Goldblatt Hyatt, E., & Franklin, C. (2022). Examining social work students' knowledge of and attitudes about abortion and curriculum coverage in social work education. *Affilia: Journal of Women & Social Work, 37*(2), 215–231.

Unit 4: Political Diversity and Social Work Education

This unit explores key issues in social work education and its relationship to political diversity. Addressing political diversity content in coursework, classroom management, and faculty to

APPENDIX

student and student to student exchanges are examined. Concepts of political transference and political countertransference are introduced.

READINGS: TEXT AND ARTICLES

Rosenwald, M. (2023). Chapter 4 in *Political ideology and social work*. Columbia University Press.

Barsky, A., Sherman, D., & Anderson, E. (2015). Social work educators' perceptions of faith-based BSW programs: Ethical inspiration and conflicts. *Journal of Social Work Values and Ethics, 12*(1), 77–87.

Bolen, R. M., & Dessel, A. B. (2013). Is discrimination against Evangelical Christians a problem in social work education? *Journal of Social Work Education, 49*, 528–547.

Flaherty, C., Ely, G. E., Meyer-Adams, N., Baer, J., & Sutphen, R. D. (2013). Are social work educators bullies? Student perceptions of political discourse in the social work classroom. *Journal of Teaching in Social Work, 33*(1), 59–74.

Galambos, C. (2009). Political tolerance, social work values, and social work education. *Journal of Teaching in Social Work, 33*(1), 59–74,

Hodge, D. R. (2014). Affirming diversity, difference, and the basic human rights of those with whom we disagree: A difficult task but worth the challenge—A reply to Bolen and Dessel. *Journal of Social Work Education, 50*(1), 153–163.

Rosenwald, M., Wiener, D. R., Smith-Osborne, A., & Smith, C. M. (2012). The place of political diversity within the social work classroom. *Journal of Social Work Education, 48*(1), 139–158.

Unit 5: Political Diversity and Social Work Practice

This unit examines the manifestation of political diversity in clinical and mezzo practice. Political countertransference and decision making is further examined and applied. The role of supervision in addressing conflicts resulting from political diversity is discussed.

APPENDIX

READINGS: TEXT AND ARTICLES

Rosenwald, M. (2023). Chapter 5 in *Political ideology and social work*. Columbia University Press.

Dessel, A. B., & Rodenborg, N. (2017b). Social workers and LGBT policies: Attitude predictors and cultural competence course outcomes *Sexuality Research and Social Policy, 14*, 17–31.

Gaston, N. R., Randall, J. M., & Kiesel, L. R. (2018). Physician-assisted suicide and Midwest social workers: Where do they stand? *Journal of Social Work in End-of-Life & Palliative Care, 14*(1), 73–92.

Jacobs, L. A., Kim, M. E., Whitfield, D. L., Gartner, R. E., Panichelli, M., Kattari, S. K., Downey, M. M., McQueen, S. S., & Mountz, S. E. (2021). Defund the police: Moving towards an anti-carceral social work. *Journal of Progressive Human Services, 32*(1), 37–62.

Jones, V. N., McElderry, C. G., & Conner, L. R. (2022). Social workers' attitudes toward reparations for African American descendants. *Journal of Social Work, 22*(4), 1031–1055.

Lennon-Dearing, R., & Delavega, E. (2016). Do social workers apply "Love Thy Neighbor as Thyself" to gay, lesbian, bisexual, and transpersons in the South? *Journal of Homosexuality, 63*(9), 1171–1193.

Rosenwald, M., & Hyde, C. (2006). Political ideology of social workers: An under explored dimension of practice. *Advances in Social Work, 7*(2), 14–26.

Saraniemi, S., Harrikari, T., Fiorentino, V., Romakkaniemi, M., & Tiitinen, L. (2022). Silenced coffee rooms—The changes in social capital within social workers' work communities during the first wave of the COVID-19 pandemic. *Challenges, 13*(1), 8.

Smith-Osborne, A., & Rosenwald, M. (2009). Exploring the relationship between religiosity and political ideology among social workers. *Journal of Religion & Spirituality in Social Work, 28*(4), 393–404.

Timbers, V. L., & Yancy, G. I. (2021). A Christian trans-affirming perspective on changes to the Patient and Affordable Care Act: Theological and practical implications for social workers of faith. *Social Work & Christianity, 48*(2), 125–136.

Winter, V. R., Kattari, S. K., Begun, S., & McKay, K. (2016). Personal and professional values: Relationships between social workers' reproductive health knowledge, attitudes, and ethical decision-making. *Journal of Social Work Values & Ethics, 13*(2), 35–46.

APPENDIX

Unit 6: The Future of Political Diversity and Social Work

This unit presents an intergroup dialogue model to reconcile political diversity in social work education and practice. Additionally, considerations for the future of political diversity and social work are examined.

READINGS: TEXT AND ARTICLES

Rosenwald, M. (2023). Chapters 6 and 7 in *Political ideology and social work*. Columbia University Press.

Dessel, A. B., & Rodenborg, N. (2017a). An evaluation of intergroup dialogue pedagogy: Addressing segregation and developing cultural competency. *Journal of Social Work Education, 53*(2), 222–239.

Everett, J. A. C., Clark, C. J., Meindl, P., Luguri, J. B., Earp, B. D., Graham, J., Ditto, P. H., & Shariff, A. F. (2021). Political differences in free will belief are associated with differences in moralization. *Journal of Personality and Social Psychology, 120*(2), 461–483.

Gurin, P., Nagda, B. A., & Zimena, X. (2013). *Dialogue across differences*. Russell Sage.

Meindl, P., Iyer, R., & Graham, J. (2019). Distributive justice beliefs are guided by whether people think the ultimate goal of society is well-being or power. *Basic & Applied Social Psychology, 41*(6), 359–385.

Segal, E. A. (2011). Social empathy: A model built on empathy, contextual understanding, and social responsibility that promotes social justice. *Journal of Social Service Research, 37*, 266–277.

Segal, E. A., & Wagaman, M. A. (2017). Social empathy as a framework for teaching social justice. *Journal of Social Work Education. 53*(2), 1–11.

ASSIGNMENTS

1. Political Transference and Political Countertransference— Role Plays and Process Recordings

   a. Create a scenario where a particular policy in which differences between a client and a social worker's political ideology may occur.

APPENDIX

    b. Enact a role play where students play a client and social worker, respectively.

    c. Continue the role play in which one student plays the social worker and another student plays the supervisor.

    d. Write a process recording in which you reflect on playing the social worker role with the client. Provide the 1) exchange between client and social worker; 2) your thoughts and feelings about what you heard from the client during the exchange (including political transference); 3) your thoughts and feelings on what you stated during the exchange (including political countertransference); and 4) questions and comments you would like to follow up with regarding supervision.

    e. Write a process recording in which you reflect on playing the *social worker role with the supervisor*. Provide the 1) exchange between the supervisor and social worker; 2) your thoughts and feelings on what you stated during the exchange; and 3) your thoughts and feelings about what you heard from the supervisor during the exchange.

    f. Provide an overall analysis of your insights into your professional development in working with clients who differ from you in political ideology.

2. Model Analysis

Drawing up your participation in A Model for Reconciling Political Diversity Among Social Workers (figure 6.1), analyze the following:

    a. An initial assessment of your political ideology on policies relating to Brint's concept of moral/military

APPENDIX

issues; egalitarian and basic system commitments, welfare state, and civil rights

b. A rationale for the formation of your political ideologies on the issues above

c. An examination of social responsibility's role in the formation of the group's varied political ideologies

d. A discussion of social empathy's role in the formation of the group's varied political ideologies

e. A reflection on participating in the intergroup dialogue with respect to your own personal development

f. A reflection on participating in the intergroup dialogue with respect to your own professional development

3. The Profession in Political Ideology Context

a. Critique the evolution of the profession with respect to its political ideology. How well has the profession historically addressed issues of social welfare policy? How has attention—or not—to issues of social welfare reflected the profession's political ideology?

b. Analyze the state of scholarship on political diversity and the profession. What more needs to be known?

c. Assess the profession's pursuit of social justice while addressing political diversity. How are these dual pursuits reconciled or could they be more fully reconciled?

ACKNOWLEDGMENTS

MANY HAVE supported me on this journey of years to produce this text. I remain grateful to my doctoral committee from the University of Maryland, where I wrote an unusual dissertation on this topic almost twenty years ago. This quintet—Drs. John Belcher, Cheryl Hyde, Bruce DeForge, Susan Zuravin, and Steve Steele provided encouragement, critique, and close edits of a topic that had not received much attention in social work literature; their support was invaluable. Over the years, my terrific colleagues from both of my teaching institutions—State University of New York, Binghamton, and Barry University—have provided me with continued inspiration to see this book to its conclusion. I am also very appreciative of the editors at Columbia University Press as well as the reviewers of the initial prospectus and final manuscript, who provided essential feedback and insight. I value the authors contained in my reference list, who have all forwarded and shaped my thinking.

ACKNOWLEDGMENTS

On a larger scale, I appreciate the politicians and policymakers who had the courage to cross party lines to make decisions for the social good. Finally, I thank Greg for his support as I shored up the time and continued focus to complete this project.

NOTES

1. THE LANDSCAPE OF POLITICAL DIVERSITY AND SOCIAL WORK

1. This chapter draws on Rosenwald (2004).
2. The three topics under "Other" do not seem relevant to political ideology per se. (The electoral politics topic does, though it relates more to the process of endorsement of policy than to any substantive policy.) Still, the remaining issues are kept to be faithful to the policy statements and for readers to determine the ultimate respective relevance of the policy statements in relation to each other as well as to the profession.
3. For social workers in countries or regions in which political ideology and political orientation *do* matter and could have an attendant "oppression," this argument looks different. For example, those practicing social work in nations impacted by the Arab Spring or in Ukraine might feel oppressed based on their marginalized political orientation and experience very real consequences of such alignment.

2. THE EVOLUTION OF THE PROFESSION IN POLITICAL CONTEXT

1. Political ideologies even among administrations of the same parties can greatly change over time. In this example, President Nixon, a

NOTES

Republican, supported a guaranteed income. This policy has not been embraced by any major Republican presidential candidates since, and even the majority of major Democratic candidates in the 2020 election did not support it.

3. RESEARCH ON POLITICAL DIVERSITY AND SOCIAL WORK

1. Sections of this chapter originally appeared in the author's dissertation.
2. An earlier version of *Social Work Speaks* was utilized at the time of the study.

7. REVISITING THE LANDSCAPE OF POLITICAL DIVERSITY IN SOCIAL WORK

1. The particular ideologies of those who draft and approve *Social Work Speaks* is unknown; therefore, it is unknown to what extent their personal political ideologies match social workers' political ideologies writ large. However, hundreds of social workers provide commentary on these statements and the Delegate Assembly is comprised of NASW members elected from their state chapters.

APPENDIX: SAMPLE SYLLABUS ON POLITICAL DIVERSITY AND SOCIAL WORK

1. This sample syllabus can be used as a Special Topics elective on Political Diversity and Social Work in a school or department of social work. Alternatively, components of this syllabus can be adapted to sections of undergraduate and graduate courses focused on practice, policy, and diversity, equity, and inclusion.

REFERENCES

Abbott, A. A. (1988). *Professional choices: Values at work.* National Association of Social Workers.

Abbott, A. A. (1999). Measuring social work values: A cross-cultural challenge for global practice. *International Social Work, 42*(4), 455–470.

Abramovitz, M. (1998). Social work and social reform: An arena of struggle. *Social Work, 43*(6), 512–526.

Anderson, J., & Carter, R. W. (2002). *Diversity perspectives for social work practice.* Allyn & Bacon.

Arnd-Caddigan, M., & Pozzuto, R. (2009). The virtuous social worker: The role of "thirdness" in ethical decision making. *Families in Society, 90*(3), 323–328.

Baradat, L. P., & Phillips, J. A. (2020). *Political ideologies: Their origins and impact* (11th ed.). Longman.

Barsky, A. E. (2022). *Ethics and values in social work* (2nd ed.). Oxford University Press.

Barsky, A., Sherman, D., & Anderson, E. (2015). Social work educators' perceptions of faith-based BSW programs: Ethical inspiration and conflicts. *Journal of Social Work Values and Ethics, 12*(1), 77–87.

Barusch, A. S. (2018). *Foundations of social policy.* Cengage.

Begun, S., Kattari, S. K., McKay, K., Ramseyer Winter, V., & O'Neill, E. (2017). Exploring U.S. social work students' sexual attitudes and abortion viewpoints. *Journal of Sex Research, 54*(6), 752–763.

REFERENCES

Berlet, C. (Ed.). (1995). *Eyes right!* South End.

Berman, A. (June 30, 2017). The Trump Administration is planning an unprecedented attack on voting rights. *The Nation*. Retrieved from https://www.thenation.com/article/the-trump-administration-is-planning-an-unprecedented-attack-on-voting-rights

Berman, L. A., & Murphy, B. A. (2012). *Approaching democracy*, 8th ed. Pearson.

Bolen, R. M., & Dessel, A. B. (2013). Is discrimination against Evangelical Christians a problem in social work education? *Journal of Social Work Education, 49*, 528–547.

Brennan, J. (2016). *Political philosophy: An introduction.* Cato Institute.

Brint, S. (1994). *In an age of experts: The changing role of professionals in politics and public life.* Princeton University Press.

Buila, S. (2010). The NASW Code of Ethics under attack: A manifestation of the culture war within the profession of social work. *Journal of Social Work Values and Ethics, 7*(2), 1–8.

Catholic Charities of the Rio Grande Valley. (2021). Catholic Social Teaching. Retrieved from https://www.catholiccharitiesrgv.org/catholic-social-teaching.shtml

Chonody, J. M., Sultzman, V., & Hippie, J. (2020). Are social work students concerned about the environment? The role of personal beliefs. *Journal of Social Work Education, 56*(4), 809–824.

Clark, E. (October 20, 2007). What does unite social workers? *The Washington Post*, A13.

Clark, E. (2008). *Dorothy I. Height and Whitney M. Young, Jr. Social Work Reinvestment Act—H.R. 5447*, Washington, DC: National Association of Social Workers. Retrieved from http://www.socialworkblog.org/advocacy/2008/02/dorothy-i-height-and-whitney-m-young-jr-social-work-reinvestment-act-hr-5447/

Cohen, M. (2008). *Political philosophy: From Plato to Mao* (2nd ed.). Pluto.

Council on Social Work Education. (2022). *Educational Policy and Accreditation Standards.* Council on Social Work Education. Retrieved from https://www.cswe.org/getmedia/94471c42-13b8-493b-9041-b30f48533d64/2022-EPAS.pdf

Csikai, E. L. (1999). The role of values and experience in determining social workers' attitudes toward euthanasia and assisted suicide. *Social Work in Health Care, 30*(1), 75–95.

Danforth, L., Hsu, H. T., & Miller, J. W. (2020). Color-blind racial attitudes among social work students: Exploration of individual and social network correlates. *Journal of Social Work Education, 56*(3), 412–427.

REFERENCES

Davis, A. (2019). Historical knowledge of oppression and racial attitudes of social work students. *Journal of Social Work Education, 55*(1), 160–175.

Deepak, A. C., Rountree, M. A., & Scott, J. (2015). Delivering diversity and social justice in social work education: The power of context. *Journal of Progressive Human Services, 26*(2), 107.

Delavega, E., Kindle, P. A., Peterson, S., & Schwartz, C. (2017). The Blame Index: Exploring the change in social work students' perceptions of poverty. *Journal of Social Work Education, 53*(4), 664–675.

Democratic National Convention. (2021). *2020 Democratic Party Platform.* Washington, DC: Retrieved from https://democrats.org/wp-content/uploads /sites/2/2020/08/2020-Democratic-Party-Platform.pdf.

Derber, C., Schwartz, W. A., & Magrass, Y. (1990). *Power in the highest degree: Professionals and the rise of a New Mandarin Order.* Oxford University Press.

Dessel, A., Bolen, R., & Shepardson, C. (2011). Can religious expression and sexual orientation affirmation coexist in social work? A critique of Hodge's theoretical, theological, and conceptual frameworks. *Journal of Social Work Education, 47*(2), 213–234.

Dessel, A. B., & Rodenborg, N. (2017a). An evaluation of intergroup dialogue pedagogy: Addressing segregation and developing cultural competency. *Journal of Social Work Education, 53*(2), 222–239.

Dessel, A. B., & Rodenborg, N. (2017b). Social workers and LGBT policies: Attitude predictors and cultural competence course outcomes. *Sexuality Research and Social Policy, 14*, 17–31.

Diamond, S. (1989). *Spiritual warfare.* South End.

DiNitto, D. M., & Cummins, L. (2007). *Social welfare* (6th ed.). Allyn & Bacon.

Dodd, S., & Mizrahi, T. (2017). Activism before and after graduation: Perspectives from three cohorts of MSW students. *Journal of Social Work Education, 53*(3), 503–519.

Dolgoff, R., & Feldstein, D. (2003). *Understanding social welfare* (6th ed.). Longman.

Ehrenreich, J. H. (1985). *The altruistic imagination: A history of social work and social policy in the United States.* Cornell University Press.

Epstein, I. (1969). *Professionalization and social work activism.* Unpublished doctoral dissertation, Columbia University.

Epstein, I. (2011). Whence and whither research on political diversity? Toward turning up the volume on a more research-based conversation. *Journal of Social Work Education, 47*(1), 163–172.

REFERENCES

Epstein, W. M. (1988). "Our town": A case study of ideology and the private social welfare sector. *Journal of Sociology and Social Welfare, 15*, 101–23.

Everett, J. A. C., Clark, C. J., Meindl, P., Luguri, J. B., Earp, B. D., Graham, J., Ditto, P. H., & Shariff, A. F. (2021). Political differences in free will belief are associated with differences in moralization. *Journal of Personality and Social Psychology, 120*(2), 461–483.

Findley, P. A., Edelstein, O. E., Pruginin, I., Reznik, A., Milano, N., & Isralowitz, R. (2021). Attitudes and beliefs about medical cannabis among social work students: Cross-national comparison. *Complementary Therapies in Medicine, 58*, 102716.

Fisher, R., Weedman, A., Alex, G., & Stout, K. D. (2001). Graduate education for social change: A study of political social workers. *Journal of Community Practice, 9*(4), 43–64.

Flaherty, C., Ely, G. E., Meyer-Adams, N., Baer, J., & Sutphen, R. D. (2013). Are social work educators bullies? Student perceptions of political discourse in the social work classroom. *Journal of Teaching in Social Work, 33*(1), 59–74.

Galambos, C. (2009). From the editor: Political tolerance, social work values, and social work education. *Journal of Social Work Education, 45*(3), 343–348.

Gaston, N. R., Randall, J. M., & Kiesel, L. R. (2018). Physician-assisted suicide and Midwest social workers: Where do they stand? *Journal of Social Work in End-of-Life & Palliative Care, 14*(1), 73–92.

Ginsberg, L. (1998). *Conservative social welfare policy*. Nelson-Hall.

Gregory, V. L., Jr., & Clary, K. L. (2022). Addressing Anti-Black racism: The roles of social work. *Smith College Studies in Social Work, 92*(1), 1–27.

Grimm, J. W., & Orten, J. D. (1973). Student attitudes toward the poor. *Social Work, 18*, 94–100.

Gurin, P., Nagda, B. A., & Zuniga, X. (2013). *Dialogue across differences*. Russell Sage.

Hansan, J. (2013). *Charity Organization Societies (1877–1893)*. Social Welfare History Project. Virginia Commonwealth University. Retrieved from https://socialwelfare.library.vcu.edu/eras/civil-war-reconstruction /charity-organization-societies-1877-1893/

Harrison, D. F., Wodarski, J. S., & Thyer, B. A. (1992). (Eds.). *Cultural diversity and social work practice*. C. C. Thomas.

Hayes, D. D. & Varley, B. K. (1965). Impact of social work education on students' values. *Social Work, 10*, 40–46.

REFERENCES

Hendershot, G. E., & Grimm, J. W. (1974). Abortion attitudes among nurses and social workers. *American Journal of Public Health, 64*(5), 438–441.

Henry, W. E., Sims, J. H., & Spray, S. L. (1971). *The fifth profession.* Jossey-Bass.

Himchak, M. V. (2011). A social justice value approach regarding physician -assisted suicide and euthanasia among the elderly. *Journal of Social Work Values and Ethics, 8*(1).

Hodge, D. R. (2003). Value differences between social workers and members of the working and middle classes. *Social Work, 48*(1), 107–119.

Hodge, D. R. (2011). Toward a learning environment that supports diversity and difference: A response to Dessel, Bolen, and Shepardson. *Journal of Social Work Education, 47*(2), 235–251.

Hodge, D. R. (2014). Affirming diversity, difference, and the basic human rights of those with whom we disagree: A difficult task but worth the challenge—A reply to Bolen and Dessel. *Journal of Social Work Education, 50*(1), 153–163.

Hoefer, R. (2019). *Advocacy practice for social justice.* (4th ed). Oxford University Press.

Hyde, C. A. (1991). *Did the New Right radicalize the women's movement? A study of change in feminist social movement organizations, 1977 to 1987.* Unpublished doctoral dissertation, The University of Michigan.

Jacobs, L. A., Kim, M. E., Whitfield, D. L., Gartner, R. E., Panichelli, M., Kattari, S. K., Downey, M. M., McQueen, S. S., & Mountz, S. E. (2021). Defund the police: Moving towards an anti-carceral social work. *Journal of Progressive Human Services, 32*(1), 37–62.

Jensen, J. P., & Bergin, A. E. (1988). Mental health values of professional therapists: A national interdisciplinary survey. *Professional Psychology: Research and Practice, 19*, 290–297.

Jones, V. N., McElderry, C. G., & Conner, L. R. (2022). Social workers' attitudes toward reparations for African American descendants. *Journal of Social Work, 22*(4), 1031–1055.

Karger, H. J., & Stoesz, D. (2018). *American social welfare policy* (8th ed.). Pearson.

Kennedy, S. C., & Tripodi, S. J. (2015). The death penalty attitudes of social work students: Current and future opportunities. *Journal of Forensic Social Work, 5*(1–3), 201–233.

Kidneigh, J. C., & Lundberg, H. W. (1958). Are social work students different? *Social Work, 3*, 57–61.

REFERENCES

Kirst-Ashman, K. K. (2007). *Introduction to social work and social welfare: Critical thinking perspectives.* Thomson Brooks/Cole.

Kirst-Ashman, K. K., & Hull, G. H., Jr. (2018). *Understanding generalist practice* (5th ed.). Cengage.

Koeske, G. F., & Crouse, M. A. (1981). Liberalism-conservatism in samples of social work students and professionals. *Social Service Review, 55,* 193–205.

Knight, K. (1999). Liberalism and conservatism. In J. P. Robinson, P. R. Shaver & L. S. Wrightsman (Eds.), *Measures of political attitudes* (pp. 59–158). Vol. 2. Academic Press.

Kuhn, T. (1996). *The structure of scientific revolutions.* University of Chicago Press.

Lennon-Dearing, R., & Delavega, E. (2016). Do social workers apply "Love Thy Neighbor as Thyself" to gay, lesbian, bisexual, and transpersons in the South? *Journal of Homosexuality, 63*(9), 1171–1193.

Lev-Weisel, R., & Friedlander, D. (1999). Role perception among social workers living in politically uncertain areas. *International Social Work, 42,* 67–86.

Linzer, N. (1999). *Resolving ethical dilemmas in social work practice.* Allyn & Bacon.

Longres, J. F. (1996). Radical social work: Is there a future? In P. R. Raffoul and C. A. McNeece (Eds.), Future issues for social work practice (pp. 229–239). Allyn and Bacon.

Lowi, T. J., & Ginsberg, B. (2002). *American government: Freedom and power* (brief 7th ed.). Norton.

Maisel, L. S., & Brewer, M. D. (2010). *Parties and elections in America* (5th ed.). Rowman & Littlefield.

Marsiglia, F. F. and Kulis, S. (2016). *Diversity, oppression, and change.* Oxford University Press.

McKenna, G. (1998). *The drama of democracy: American government and politics* (3rd ed.). McGraw Hill.

McLeod, D. L., & Meyer, H. J. (1967). A study of the values of social workers. In F. J. Thomas (Ed.), *Behavioral Science for Social Workers* (pp. 401–416). Free Press.

McPherson, J., Villarreal-Otálora, T., & Kobe, D. (2021). Injustice in their midst: Social work students' awareness of immigration-based discrimination in higher education. *Journal of Social Work Education, 57*(1), 55–69.

Meindl, P., Iyer, R., & Graham, J. (2019). Distributive justice beliefs are guided by whether people think the ultimate goal of society is well-being or power. *Basic & Applied Social Psychology, 41*(6), 359–385.

REFERENCES

Mizrahi, T., & Dodd, S. J. (2013). MSW students' perspectives on social work goals and social activism. *Journal of Social Work Education, 49*(4), 580–600.

National Association of Social Workers. (2015). *NASW supports the Obama Administration call to ban the use of conversion therapy for youth.* National Association of Social Workers. Retrieved from http://www.socialworkblog .org/advocacy/2015/04/nasw-supports-the-obama-administration-call-to -ban-the-use-of-conversion-therapy-for-youth/

National Association of Social Workers. (2016). *NASW Statement on Donald J. Trump Election as 45th U.S. President.* National Association of Social Workers. Retrieved from https://www.socialworkers.org/News/News-Releases /ID/88/%22

National Association of Social Workers. (2019). *Social Work Reinvestment Act.* National Association of Social Workers. Retrieved from https://www.social-workers.org/Advocacy/Policy-Issues/Social-Work-Reinvestment-Act

National Association of Social Workers. (2021a). *Code of Ethics.* National Association of Social Workers. Retrieved from https://www.socialworkers.org /About/Ethics/Code-of-Ethics/Code-of-Ethics-English

National Association of Social Workers. (2021b). *Social Work Speaks: NASW policy statements 2021–2023.* (2021) (12th ed.). National Association of Social Workers.

National Association of Social Workers. (2021c). *2021 Blueprint of Federal Social Policy Priorities.* National Association of Social Workers. Retrieved from https://www.socialworkers.org/Advocacy/Policy-Issues/2021-Blueprint -of-Federal-Social-Policy-Priorities

National Association of Social Workers. (2021d). *Interactive timeline.* National Association of Social Workers. Retrieved from https://www.socialworkers .org/news/facts/interactive-timeline-of-social-work-and-nasw

National Association of Social Workers. (2021e). *NASW calls for President Trump to be removed from office.* Retrieved from https://www.socialworkers.org /News/News-Releases/ID/2271/NASW-calls-for-President-Trump-to-be -removed-from-office

O'Connors, K., & Sabato, L. J. (2000). *American government: Continuity and change.* Longman.

Ostrander, J., Lane, S., McClendon, J., Hayes, C., & Smith, T. (2017). Collective power to create political change: Increasing the political efficacy and engagement of social workers. *Journal of Policy Practice, 16*(3), 261–275.

REFERENCES

Park, Y., Torres, M., Bhuyan, R., Ao, J., Graves, L., & Rundle, A. (2022). Social workers' perceptions of structural inequality and immigrant threat: Results from a national survey. *Journal of Social Work Education, 58*(3), 449–471.

Peter G. Peterson Foundation. (2021). *Here's everything the Federal government has done to respond to the Coronavirus so far.* Retrieved from https://www.pgpf.org/blog/2021/03/heres-everything-congress-has-done-to-respond-to-the-coronavirus-so-far

Planned Parenthood. (2021). *Mission.* Retrieved from https://www.plannedparenthood.org/about-us/who-we-are/mission

Rawls, J. (1971). *A theory of justice.* Harvard University Press.

Reamer, F. G. (2005). Ethical and legal standards in social work: Consistency and conflict. *Families in Society, 86*(2), 163–169.

Reamer, F. G. (2006). Eye on ethics. *Social Work Today.* Retrieved from https://www.socialworktoday.com/news/eoe_0906.shtml

Reamer, F. G. (2022). *Ethical decision-making: A practical strategy.* Behavioral Health CE. Retrieved from https://behavioralhealthce.com/index.php?option=com_courses&task=view&cid=171

Reeser, L., & Epstein, I. (1990). *Professionalization and activism in social work: The sixties, the eighties, and the future.* Columbia University Press.

Reid, C., & LeDrew, R. A. (2013). The burden of being "employable": Underpaid and unpaid work and women's health. *Affilia, 28*(1), 79–93.

Reisch, M. (2022). *Social policy and social justice* (4th ed.). Cognella.

Reisch, M., & Jani, J. S. (2012). The new politics of social work practice: Understanding context to promote change. *British Journal of Social Work, 42*(6), 1132–1150.

Reisch, M., & Rohde, L. (2000). The future of social work in the United States: Implications for field education. *Journal of Social Work Education, 36*(2), 201–214.

Reisch, M., & Staller, K. M. (2011). Teaching social welfare history and social welfare policy from a conflict perspective. *Journal of Teaching in Social Work, 31*(2), 131–144.

Republican National Committee. (2021). *Resolution regarding the Republican platform.* Republican National Committee. Retrieved from https://wvgop.org/wp-content/uploads/2021/03/Resolution_Platform_2020.pdf

Ringstad, R. R. (2014). Political diversity among social work students. *Journal of Social Work Values and Ethics, 11*(2), 13–22.

REFERENCES

Robbins, S. P., Chatterjee, P., Canda, E. R., & Leibowitz, G. S. (2019). *Contemporary human behavior theory: A critical perspective for social work* (4th ed.). Pearson.

Rodenborg, N. A., & Boisen, L. A. (2013) Aversive racism and intergroup contact theories: Cultural competence in a segregated world, *Journal of Social Work Education, 49*(4), 564–579.

Rodenborg, N., & Bosch, L. A. (2007). Intergroup dialogue: A group work method for diverse groups. *Encyclopedia for Social Work with Groups* (pp.1–7). Retrieved from http://web.augsburg.edu/socialwork/msw/pdfs /dialogue.pdf

Rom, M. C., Hidaka, M., & Walker, R. B. (2022). *Introduction to political science*. Open Textbook Library.

Rosenwald, M. (2004). *Exploring political ideologies of licensed social workers*. Unpublished dissertation, University of Maryland at Baltimore.

Rosenwald, M. (2006a). Exploring the political ideologies of licensed social workers. *Social Work Research, 30*(2), 121–126.

Rosenwald, M. (2006b). A part versus apart: Exploring the relationship between social workers' political ideology and their professional affiliation. *Journal of Social Work Values and Ethics, 3*(2), 61–77.

Rosenwald, M., Baird, J., & Williams, J. (2023). A social work model of historical trauma. *British Journal of Social Work, 53*(1), 621–636.

Rosenwald, M., & Hyde, C. (2006). Political ideology of social workers: An under explored dimension of practice. *Advances in Social Work, 7*(2), 14–26.

Rosenwald, M., Wiener, D. R., Smith-Osborne, A., & Smith, C. M. (2012). The place of political diversity within the social work classroom. *Journal of Social Work Education, 48*(1), 139–158.

Rubinstein, G. (1994). Political attitudes and religiosity levels of Israeli psychotherapy practitioners and students. *American Journal of Psychotherapy, 48*, 441–454.

Sagi, A., & Dvir, R. (1993). Value biases of social workers in custody disputes. *Children and Youth Services Review, 15*, 27–42.

Saraniemi, S., Harrikari, T., Fiorentino, V., Romakkaniemi, M., & Tiitinen, L. (2022). Silenced coffee rooms—The changes in social capital within social workers' work communities during the first wave of the COVID-19 pandemic. *Challenges, 13*(1), 8.

Sargent, L. T. (1995). *Contemporary political ideologies: A comparative analysis*. Harcourt Brace.

REFERENCES

Segal, E. A. (2011). Social empathy: A model built on empathy, contextual understanding, and social responsibility that promotes social justice. *Journal of Social Service Research, 37,* 266–277.

Segal, E. A., & Wagaman, M. A. (2017). Social empathy as a framework for teaching social justice. *Journal of Social Work Education. 53*(2), 1–11.

Sheridan, M. J., Wilmer, C. M., & Atcheson, L. (1994). Inclusion of content on religion and spirituality in the social work curriculum: A study of faculty views. *Journal of Social Work Education, 30,* 363–376.

Shulman, L. (2008). Supervision. *Encyclopedia of Social Work.* Oxford University Press.

Smith-Osborne, A., & Rosenwald, M. (2009). Exploring the relationship between religiosity and political ideology among social workers. *Journal of Religion & Spirituality in Social Work, 28*(4), 393–404.

Specht, H., & Courtney, M. E. (1994). *Unfaithful angels.* Free Press.

Timbers, V. L., & Yancy, G. I. (2021). A Christian trans-affirming perspective on changes to the Patient and Affordable Care Act: Theological and practical implications for social workers of faith. *Social Work & Christianity, 48*(2), 125–136.

Trattner, W. I. (1999). *From poor law to welfare state* (6th ed.) Free Press.

University of Michigan. (2022). *The Program on Intergroup Relations.* University of Michigan. Retrieved from https://igr.umich.edu/article/institute

Valutis, S., Rubin, D., & Bell, M. (2012). Professional socialization and social work values: Who are we teaching? *Social Work Education, 31*(8), 1046–1057.

Varley, B. K. (1963). Socialization in social work education. *Social Work, 8,* 102–109.

Varley, B. K. (1968). Social work values: Changes in value commitments of students from admission to MSW graduation. *Education in Social Work, 11,* 67–76.

Van Soest, D., & Garcia, B. (2008). *Diversity education for social justice.* Council on Social Work Education.

Virginia Commonwealth University. (2021). *Settlement Houses.* VCU Libraries Social History Project. Virginia Commonwealth University. Retrieved from http://www.socialwelfarehistory.com/organizations/settlement-houses/

Virginia Commonwealth University. (2021). *Social Welfare History Project.* Virginia Commonwealth University. Retrieved from: http://www.social welfarehistory.com/

Wagner, D. (1990). *The quest for a radical profession.* University Press of America.

REFERENCES

Watkins, J. M. (October 16, 2007). *CSWE response to the Washington Post: Social justice and accreditation standards* [Electronic mailing list message]. Council on Social Work Education.

Werley, H. H., Ager, J. W., Rosen, R. A. H., & Shea, F. P. (1973). Professionals and birth control: Student and faculty attitudes. *Family Planning Perspective, 5*, 42–49.

Wertheimer, A. (2002). Liberty, coercion, and the limits of the state. (38–59). In Simon, R. L. (Ed.). *The Blackwell Guide to Social and Political Philosophy.* Blackwell.

Westen, D. (2007). *The political brain.* Public Affairs.

Will, G. F. (October 14, 2007). Code of coercion. *The Washington Post.*

Winter, V. R., Kattari, S. K., Begun, S., & McKay, K. (2016). Personal and professional values: Relationships between social workers' reproductive health knowledge, attitudes, and ethical decision-making. *Journal of Social Work Values & Ethics, 13*(2), 35–46.

Witt, H., Younes, M. K., Goldblatt Hyatt, E., & Franklin, C. (2022). Examining social work students' knowledge of and attitudes about abortion and curriculum coverage in social work education. *Affilia: Journal of Women & Social Work, 37*(2), 215–231.

Woodcock, R. (2008). Preamble, purpose, and ethical principles sections of the NASW code of ethics: A preliminary analysis. *Families in Society, 89*(4), 578–586.

Yip, K. (2006). Developing social work students' reflectivity in cultural indigenization of mental health practice. *Reflective Practice, 7*(3), 393–408.

INDEX

Abbott, A. A., 6, 63, 66, 68–69, 70; Professional Opinion Scale of, 183–184; on values, 72

abortion, beliefs of social workers on, 82, 93, 97, 99–100, 105; impact on practice and, 116

Abramovitz, M., 57

ACA. *See* Patient Protection and Affordable Care Act

accreditation standards, for social work, 24, 88–89

activism, social workers and, 154, 175–176, 181–182

Addams, Jane, 40–41, 45–46

advocacy: CSWE on, 28; for resources of agencies, 138–139

AFDC. *See* Aid to Families with Dependent Children

age, inconclusive effect on political ideology of, 68

agency employment, mission congruence and, 136

agency practice, political diversity and, 135–136

Aid to Families with Dependent Children (AFDC), 56

American Association of University Professors, 29

American Reinvestment and Recovery Act (ARRA), 58

American Rescue Plan (ARPA), 59

Americans with Disabilities Act, 55

anti-abortion social work students, study of Brint on, 82

anti-Muslim rhetoric, of Trump administration, 58–59

applied nature, of social work profession, 114–115

ARPA. *See* American Rescue Plan

ARRA. *See* American Reinvestment and Recovery Act

INDEX

assumptions, by social work faculty, 109

Atcheson, L., 69

bachelor of social work (BSW), political affiliation and, 63–64, 66

Baradat, L. P., 7

Bell, M., 108

Bertha Capen Reynolds Society, 55–56

Biblical literalism, 12

Biden, Joe, 59, 110, 190; championing by NASW of, 60

bipartisan support, evidence of, 189–190

blame for circumstances, assignment of, 144–146; discussion of in intergroup dialogues, 149–150

block grants, of Reagan administration, 54

bodily autonomy, social work policy on, 102–103

Boisen, L. A., 181

Bolen, R. M., 26, 107

Brint, S., 13, 39, 44–45, 46, 49; basic system commitments, 100; on employment status influence on political beliefs of, 70–71; model of political diversity of, 90; on morality issues, 81–82, 121–122

Brooker, Emily, 29

BSW. *See* bachelor of social work

Buila, S., 26

Build Back Better program, of Biden, 174

Bush, George H. W., 54–55

Bush, George W., 57–58

capitalism: charity organization societies on, 38; critiques from New Left ideology on, 8, 105; New Right ideology on, 12; settlement houses and, 42–43

CAPTA. *See* Child Abuse Prevention and Treatment Act

CARES. *See* Coronavirus Aid, Relief, and Economic Security Act

Carter, Jimmy, 53

Catholic Charities of the Rio Grande Valley, mission statement of, 137

Catholic student, Social Welfare Policy course and, 1–2

Census of United States, listing of social work in, 47

challenge of belief, in intergroup dialogues, 150

change through government, conservative ideology on, 10–11

charity organization societies (COS), 35–36, 37–40; hiring of staff by, 45; political context of, 43–44; settlement houses as response to, 41, 43; settlement houses contrasted with, *44*

charity roots, of social work profession, 33–34

Child Abuse Prevention and Treatment Act (CAPTA), 53

Children's Bureau, of U.S., 50

child welfare policies, 18

child welfare workers, attitudes on custody decisions of, 71

Christian social workers, nontraditional notions of gender and, 84

■ 220 ■

INDEX

circumstantial difficulties, liberal ideology on, 141

civil liberties, 13

civil rights: of prisoners, 21; views of social workers on, 82

Civil Rights Act, 51

civil rights movement, 50–51

Clark, Betsy, 31

classroom management, differing politics and, 105–106, 158–159, 168–169

client assignment, necessity of social worker to accept, 134–135, 169–170

client beliefs, respect of by social worker, 158–159, 172

client empowerment, social workers in study of Rosenwald on, 75

client mobilization, shift from service coordination of, 52

client reaction, awareness of student of, 93, 96–97

client relationships, use of self in, 130

clients with differing beliefs, difficulty of social workers with, 71, 154, 169–170

climate change, NASW position on, 163–164

clinical practice, political ideology and, 71, 114–115, 158–159; strategies for addressing, 171

Clinton, William, 56–57

"Code Of Coercion" (Wills), 27–28

Code of Ethics (National Association of Social Workers), 25–26, 28–29, 90; belief in political ideology and, 75; on prejudice, 170; social justice and, 118, 157, 160

Cohen, M., 3–4

collective caregiving roles, 39–40

Columbia University, first social work course at, 36, 45

common ground, with other political beliefs, 107, 147

community-based clinics, family planning and, 2

community chests, settlement houses and, 41–42

Community Mental Health Act, 51

competency in diversity, of EPAS, 89

Comprehensive Child Care Act, veto, 53

conception issues, 99–100

Congress, bipartisan collaboration in, 189–191

Congressional Social Work Caucus, 60

conservative ideology, 10–11; critique of social work profession for, 185–186; deservingness policy of, 140, 145; early social work and, 39, 47, 184–185; respect of worker belief in, 190–191; social work training problems and, 109; study of Rosenwald and, 156–157

conservative perspective: vignette #1, 123; vignette #2, 124; vignette #3, 125–126; vignette #4, 127

conservative populism, 7

conservative social workers, treatment of by colleagues, 147

conservative social work students, on treatment by peers, 78, 87–88, 105

conspiracy theories, clients and, 172

contextual understanding, 143

cornerstone of social work practice, social work as, 22

■ 221 ■

INDEX

Coronavirus Aid, Relief, and Economic Security Act (CARES), 59
COS. *See* charity organization societies
Council on Social Work Education (CSWE), 24–25, 28, 30–31, 52, 88–89
coursework, political diversity examples in, 90, 92
Courtney, M. E., 47
COVID-19, 59, 85, 161
critical thinking, encouragement of, 109–111
Crouse, M. A., 67
CSWE. *See* Council on Social Work Education

DACA. *See* Deferred Action for Childhood Arrivals
death penalty, views of social workers on, 82
"Declaration of Principles" (American Association of University Professors), 29
Defense of Marriage Act, 56
Deferred Action for Childhood Arrivals (DACA), 58–59, 84–85
Delegate Assembly, of NASW, 5
democratic liberalism, 6–7, 9
Democratic Party platform, *Social Work Speaks* policies compared with, 23–24, 26, 175
Democratic Party presidential primary, of 2020, 110
Democrats, majority of social workers as, 62–63, 78–79, 185

demographic correlates, of political ideology, 68–69, 72–73, 76–77
demographic factors, activism and, 81
Department of Education, start of, 53
Department of Energy, start of, 53
deservingness policy, of conservative ideology, 140, 145
Dessel, A. B., 26, 107
development milestones, political views on, 99
differing politics, extended discussion and, 107, 146–147, 158–159
dignity client, respect for, 117–118
directors of social welfare agencies, political philosophy of, 65
disaster relief, bipartisan support for, 140
Discourse on Inequality, The (Rousseau), 3–4
discrimination on LGBT issues: NASW position on, 166; social worker views on, 83–84, 115, 159
distributive justice, 118–119, 120–121
diversity, representation and, 75
diversity knowledge on race and ethnicity, political diversity contrasted with, 21–22
diversity statement, of Emotional Policy and Accreditation Standards, 24
divisive climate, social work and, 152–153
Dix, Dorothea, 34–35
Dobbs v. Jackson Women's Health Organization (court case), 82

■ 222 ■

INDEX

Dodd, S., 80–81, 88, 185–186

Dolgoff, R., 35, 38–39, 186

drug use, social worker views on, 145

Earned Income Tax Credit (EITC), 54–55

economic components of political ideologies, social and, 13, *14*, *15*, *16*, *7*

economic inequality, NASW position on, 165

Economic Opportunity Act (1964), 51

economic systems, lack of research found on social research views on, 86

education, social workers in, 62

Educational Policy and Accreditation Standards (EPAS), 88–89

education policies, 18

efficiency, focus of settlement houses on, 42–43

EITC. *See* Earned Income Tax Credit

"Electoral Politics" policy, of *Social Work Speaks*, 26–27

Eliot, Martha, 49–50

emotion, policymaking and, 115

Emotional Policy and Accreditation Standards, of Council on Social Work Education, 24–25

empathy: in classroom discussions, 105–106; in intergroup dialogues, *147*

employment status, political beliefs and, 70–71

end-of-life care, 100, 122–123

energy bill, fund for assistance with, 138–139

environmental concerns, social worker views on, 85

EPAS. *See* Educational Policy and Accreditation Standards

Epstein, I., 62, 63, 64, 65, 80; on perceived liberal bias of social work, 185

equal opportunities, NASW position on, 165

Equal Rights Act, 51

ethical conflicts, based on political diversity, *122*

ethical decision making, 108–109, 130–131, 169

ethical dilemmas: practice courses and, 95–96; social work practice and, 117, 121

ethical framework, for social work practice, 117, 141

ethical principles, political ideology and, *119*

ethnicity, social responsibility and in study of Ringstad, 78–79

Everett, J. A. C., 144–145

Evolutionary Marxists, 8

experience level, of intergroup dialogues, 150

explanation stage, of intergroup dialogue, 149–150

exposure level, of intergroup dialogues, 149

extended discussion, differing politics and, 107, 146–147

faculty, political questions and, 103, 158

Family and Medical Leave Act, 56–57

• 223 •

INDEX

Family Assistance Plan, proposal of Nixon, 53

Family Support Act, 54–55

Federal Emergency Relief Act, 49–50

federal government: devolution of social services of, 54; social welfare and, 48–50, 154, 160, 167

Feldstein, D., 35, 38–39, 186

Felkner, William, 30

female social worker beliefs, male social workers contrasted with, 68

feminism, New Left ideology and, 8–9

field education, 90, 92–95

field placements, research on workers in, 182–183

first stage, of intergroup dialogues, 149

Fisher, R., 64–65, 77

Flaherty, C., 78, 79

Flexner, Abraham, 46

food stamp pilot program, 51

Ford, Gerald, 53

for-profit sector roles, conservative ideology on, 11

fourth stage, of intergroup dialogues, 151

free will: conservative ideology and, 144–145; discussion in intergroup dialogues of, 149–150

Freud, Sigmund, 46–47, 50, 181–182

Friedlander, D., 71

Fuiten, Sandra, 30

funding stream, of settlement houses, 41–42

Galambos, C., 24–25, 133, 170

gender identity discussion group, 147

general public, social worker political ideology compared with, 65–67

General Social Survey, study of Hodge and, 63–64, 67

genetic research, position of NASW on, 100

genetic testing, 99–100

government assistance, Pierce on, 35

government entitlement programs, 9–10

government responsibilities: Pierce on, 34–35; Rousseau on, 3–4

gradual change, moderate ideology on, 10

Great Depression, 48–50

Great Society, of Johnson administration, 51

group rules, for classroom discussions, 106

gun control legislation, passage of by Biden administration Congress, 189

Gurtee, S. Humphreys, 37

harm, 119, 141, 155–156; differing ideas of, 120–121; self-determinism and, 121, 132–133; in vignette #1, 123; in vignette #2, 124; in vignette #3, 125–126; in vignette #4, 127

healthcare settings, social work dilemmas and, 2, 85

healthcare worker beliefs, social worker beliefs compared with, 66

health policies, 18, 162

Henry, W. E., 63

Hidaka, M., 7

HIV/AIDS, under Reagan administration, 54

■ 224 ■

INDEX

Hodge, D. R., 26, 63, 67, 105–106, 107
Hoefer, R., 118–119
homeland security, administration of George W. Bush on, 57–58
homelessness, NASW position, 163
homophobic client, sympathetic intern and, 94
homosexual foster home assignment, Booker and, 29
Hopkins, Harry, 49–50
Hull House, Chicago, 40
human behavior courses, 99–100
Hurricane Ian, collaboration of Biden and DeSantis on, 190
Hyde, C., 61–62, 71–72, 113–115, 120; study of, 73–77

ideological stance, of social work profession, 33–34
IGD. *See* intergroup dialogue
immigrant children, separation from parents of, 59
immigrants from Muslim majority countries, attempted ban by Trump administration of, 58–59
immigration status: NASW position on, 165; social worker views on, 84–85
independent variable, treatment of political ideology as, 72
individual "failings," deterministic understanding of, 38–39
individual freedom: beliefs in study of Rosenwald and Hyde, 74; MSW graduate beliefs on, 66
individualism, social equality issues and, 13

individual rights, conservative ideology on, 11
individuals, dividends for, 140
inequities, social worker effort against, 154
Inflation Reduction Act, 59
instructor awareness, of political expression, 104–105, 168–169
insurrection, of January 6, 2021, 60
intergroup dialogue (IGD), 107, 142, 146–147, *148*; challenge of belief in, 150; discussion of free will in, 149–150; experience level of, 150; explanation stage, of, 149–150; exposure level of, 149; first stage of, 149; fourth stage of, 151; political diversity and, 147; second stage of, 149–150; third stage of, 150

Jacobs, L. A., 83
Jani, J. S., 185
Johnson, Lyndon B., 51

Kennedy, John F., 51
Kirst-Ashman, K. K., 26
Koeske, G. F., 67

Lee, Porter, 46–47
Legislative Action Network, 55
legislative advocacy, 99
legislative agenda, of NASW, 108, 159–167; alignment with Democratic party platform of, 175–176; level of agreement of social workers with, 174–177; reflection of social work educators on, 175–176

INDEX

legislature lobby assignment, Felkner and Fuiten on, 30

legitimacy, of social work profession, 49

Lenroot, Katharine, 49–50

level of education, liberal ideology and, 70

Lev-Weisel, R., 71

liberal ideology, 9–10; assumed espousal of social work profession, 23–26, 109, 184–186; critique of social work profession for, 185–186; disagreements within, 110; history of social work and, 184–185; New Deal and, 49; settlement houses and, 41–43; social workers in study of Rosenwald on, 75, 156; of social work of 1960s, 51–52; of social work of 1970s, 55; social work students and, 79–80, 109

liberal perspective: vignette #1, 122–123; vignette #2, 124; vignette #3, 125–126; vignette #4, 127

libertarianism, 6–7

Likert Scale of political ideology, 74

Linzer, N., 71

lobbying, *Social Work Speaks* policy statements and, 160

lobbyist, of CSWE, 52

lower federal court judges, NASW position on, 165

macro causes, 39

macro change, 50

macro level, 98–99

macro practice, 52, 159–160, 174–175

maltreated children, NASW position on, 166

Manual for Visitors Among the Poor (Philadelphia Society), 38

marginalized populations, difficulties of, 154

masks, politicization of, 85

Master of Social Work (MSW), 66; study of Mizrahi & Dodd of, 80

McLeod, D. L., 68, 69–70

medical cannabis, social worker views on, 85

Medicare Part D, 58

mental health services, access to, 162

mental health worker beliefs, social worker beliefs compared with, 67

mental illness support, Dix on, 34–35

Meyer, H. J., 68, 69–70

mezzo level, studies on, 65, 98, 135–136

micro level, 96–97, 114–115

middle-class white values, settlement houses and, 42–43

militarism, 45

military, critique from New Left ideology on, 8

minimum wage, *Social Work Speaks* policy on, 102–103

minority beliefs, social work training programs and, 110–111

mission congruence, agency employment and, 136

mission to protect citizens, of government, 9–10

Missouri State University, 29

Mizrahi, T., 80–81, 88, 185–186

moderate ideology: in study of Ringwald, 79–80; in study of Rosenwald, 157

■ 226 ■

INDEX

morality: beliefs political ideology and, 81–82, 144–145; in political ideologies, 13

moral judgments, of poverty, 38

moral wrongdoing, political ideologies and, 145

MSW. *See* Master of Social Work

Muslim student, xenophobic client and, 94

NAS. *See* National Association of Scholars

NASW. *See* National Association of Social Workers

National Association of Scholars (NAS), 27–28, 30

National Association of Social Workers (NASW), 1–2, 28, 31, 51–52, 75; agenda of, 108, 159–167, 174–177; criticism by social workers of, 76, 156; level of agreement of social workers with, 174–175; litmus test for membership on board of, 175

Neighborhood Guild, the, 40

neoliberal views: of Clinton, 56; Reisch & Jani on, 185

New Christian Right, 12

newcomers to cities, assistance for, 36–37

New Deal, 48–49; social work response to, 50

New Federalism program, of Reagan administration, 54

New Left: challenge of taking conservative clients of, 135; criticism of eligibility guideline of, 140; lack of studies of social

workers and, 64; in study of Rosenwald, 156; vignette #4 and, 125–126

New Right, 6–7, 11–12; challenges of taking liberal clients of, 135; lack of research on social workers and, 64

Nixon, Richard, 53

No Child Left Behind Act, 58

No Party Affiliation (NPA), 183

Obama, Barack, 58; championing by NASW of, 60

Occupational Safety and Health Act (OSHA), 53

older adults, NASW position on, 163

opioid addiction, bipartisan support for, 189

oppression, discussion of, 149–150, 179–180

oppressive history, diversity variables and, 23

oppressive institutions, New Left ideology on, 8

OSHA. *See* Occupational Safety and Health Act

Ostrander, J., 81

oversimplification of political ideologies, problems with, 109

paid work, work in home contrasted with, 126–127

PAS. *See* physician-assisted suicide

Patient Protection and Affordable Care Act (ACA), 58

patriarchal family roles, 12

people with disabilities, NASW position on, 166

■ 227 ■

INDEX

Perkins, Frances, 49–50
Perlman, Helen Harris, 52
permanent safety net, for citizens, 48–49
personal difference, COS movement on, 39
personal growth, risk encouragement and, 87–88
Personal Responsibility and Work Opportunity Act (PWORA), 56
Philadelphia Society for Organizing Charitable Relief and Repressing Mendicancy, 38
Phillips, J. A., 7
physician-assisted suicide (PAS): renal failure client and, 122–123, 132; views of social workers on, 82, 100
Pierce, Franklin, 34–35
Planned Parenthood: Clinton administration and, 56–57; mission statement of, 136–137
polarizing issues, social worker views on, 21
police, social workers and, 83
policy change, political process and, 4
policy courses, 102
policy positions: by economic and social components, *19, 20*; social worker views on, 154
policy statements, of NASW, 5–6, 82
"Policy Statement Topic Areas" (National Association of Social Workers), 13
Political Action for Candidate Endorsement and Education, 55
political affiliation, as measure of ideology in studies, 73

political beliefs: pushing on client of, 173–174; social worker actions and, 154; views on discrimination and, 84
political countertransference, *92,* 92–93, 95–97, 115–116, 128–129; clinical practice and, 171–172; new social workers and, 158–159
political diversity, 5–7, 178; addressing of within social work profession, 167–168, 186–187; agency practice and, 135–136; clinical practice and, 71, 114–115, 158–159, 171, 181–182; complexity of, 12–13, 21, 31–32, 183–184; conflict and, 103–104; coursework and, 90, 92; encouraged respect for, 89; historical research on, 61–62; intergroup dialogues and, 147, 149; model for reconciling, 142–143, *143*; need for more research on, 178–179, *179*; at organizational level, 136, 173; Rosenwald on, 186; social work education and, 77–80, 87–88, 110–112, 168–169, 180–181; social work practice and, 116–117, 152–153; study of Rosenwald and Hyde on, 73–74
political ideology expression, allowance of, in social worker education, 104–105, 110–111, 168–169
political litmus test, for potential social workers, 88
Political machines, goods-for-votes system of, 36–37
political oppression, other oppressions compared with, 21–23

■ 228 ■

INDEX

political party affiliation, as indicator of political ideology, 183–184
political permeability, 103
political philosophy, 6–12; social work instructors and, 104; studies of social workers and, 62–63
political positions: ability to defend of, 111; government regulations for agencies and, 138–139
political prejudice, 23, 107, 158, 169–170, 173–174
political social work training, study of Ostrander on, 81
political tolerance, democratic societies and, 25
political transference, 94, 95
political views: alignment with agency and, 137–138, 173; social worker awareness of, 115–116, 128–130
politics: Cohen on, 3–4; as taboo topic in social work, 23–24
politikos (pertaining to city), 3
poverty: as individual issue, 37–38; under Reagan administration, 54
practical reflexivity, 106–107, 129–130, *131*, 134
practice, effect of political ideology of, 73, 76, 77, 113–114
practice, social workers in, 62
practice courses, 95–96
prejudice, political, 23, 107, 158, 169–170, 173–174
private charities, conservative ideology on, 140
privatized social service delivery system, during Industrial Revolution, 36

pro-choice student, pregnant teenager and, 97
pro-family values, of New Right ideology, 12
professional affiliation, political ideology and, 74–75, 77
professional correlates, of social workers, 70–71, 72–73, 76–77
professionalization, of social work profession, 47, 50, 181–182
Professional Opinion Scale, of social workers, 6, 63, 73–74, 78, 183–184
professional participation, political ideology and, 73
professional socialization, political ideology, 157–159, 167–168
pro-life student, abortion-seeking client and, 97
Protestant Work Ethic, 39–40, 140
PRWORA. *See* Personal Responsibility and Work Opportunity Act
psychiatric casework, early social work and, 47
psychiatric social workers, study of Henry of, 63
psychiatrist political affiliations, social workers compared with, 67
psychological treatment, social work and, 46–47, 50
public child welfare, 21
public perfection, of social work profession, 27

race, political ideology and, 68
race or ethnicity, political view contrasted with in client interactions, 21–22

■ 229 ■

INDEX

Race to the Top program, of Obama administration, 58
racism policies: NASW position on, 164, 165; social worker views on, 83
racist beliefs, liberal social worker response to, 121
radical ideology, prediction of activism and, 80
radical social workers, study of Wagner on, 64
range of political ideology expression, allowance of, 104–105, 110–111
rank and file level, of study of Dodd and Mizrahi, 186
Rawls, J., 118–119, 140, 154
reaction to client, awareness of student of, 93, 96–97
Reagan, Ronald, 53–54
Reagan administration ideology, social welfare agencies and, 65
Reaganomics, 54
Reagan Revolution, 53–54
Reamer, F. G., 133
recent scholarship, on political ideology, 73–74
Reeser, L., 62, 63, 64, 80
reflective environment, in social worker education, 169
reflectivity, 115–116, 129–130, 172
reform-mindedness, professionalization contrasted with, 55
regulations, of agency bureaucracy, 138–139
Reisch, M., 185

religious beliefs of social workers: attitudes on euthanasia and, 71; political beliefs and, 69–70, 74, 76, 113–114, 156
reparations to African Americans, social worker views on, 83
representation by NASW, study of Rosenwald on, 75–76
reproductive rights, 99–100
required written response, of Booker, 29–30
research: courses, 101–102; measures for future, 183–184; methods for future, 182–183; on political ideology lack of, 71–73; questions political perspectives of, 101–102
resources: allocation of, 138–139; redistribution of, 118–119, 121
Response of Social Work to the Depression, The (government publication), 49
Revolutionary Marxists, 8
rhetorical attack, on U.S. Congresswomen, 59
Rhode Island College, 30
Richmond, Mary, 45–46
right-wing funding for social welfare organization, differing student views and, 98
Ringstad, R. R., 78, 88
Rodenborg, N., 181
Roe v. Wade (court case), 82
Rohde, L., 185
role-play, differences in values and, 97
Rom, M. C., 7
Roosevelt, Franklin Delano, 48

■ 230 ■

INDEX

Rosenwald, Mitchell, 25, 61–62, 113–115, 120; on harm, 155–156; on political diversity, 186; study on political ideology and social work, 73–77

Rousseau, Jean-Jacques, 3–4

Rubin, D., 108

Ryan White Act, 54

safety net, government as, 9–10

same-sex couple, social worker and, 1

sampling strategy, for future research, 182–183

Sanders, Bernie, 110

SCHIP. *See* State Children's Health Insurance Program

School of Social Work, at Rhode Island College, 30

second stage, of intergroup dialogue, 149–150

Segal, E. A., 144

self-assessment, 106–107

self-determinism, 39–41, 108–109, 117–120, 131; blame for circumstances and, 145–146; client relationships and, 174; harm and, 121, 132–133; reconciling with social justice of, 142; social worker beliefs and, 174

self-identity, client relationships and, 130

separation of practice from political ideology, conservative social workers on, 76

service coordination, shift to client mobilization of, 52

settlement houses, 35–36, 40; charity organizations contrasted with,

44; political context of, 43–44; programs community chests and, 41–42; protest against World War I of, 45–46; responses to COS system as, 41, 43

sexual orientation, acknowledgment of, 84

Sexual Orientation Change/ Conversion Efforts (SOCE), 94

Shepardson, C., 107

Sheridan, M. J., 70

Smith-Osborne, A., 76

SNAP. *See* Supplemental Nutrition Assistance Program

SOCE. *See* Sexual Orientation Change/Conversion Efforts

social components of political ideologies, economic and, 13, *14, 15, 16, 17*

social conservatism, 6–7

Social Construct, The (Rousseau), 3–4

Social Democrats, 8

social empathy framework, 142–143

social inequities, liberal ideologies on, 9

social institutions, radical views and, 2

socialism, 6–7

social isolation, NASW position on, 163

social justice: differing views on, 108, 117, 187; label social workers and, 64–65, 100; political ideology as perspective of, 154–157; reconciling of social determinism of, 142; social work practice and, 118–119, 132–133; social work training programs and, 109–110

INDEX

social movements, 162

social policies, 18

social progress, New Right ideology on, 11–12

social reform, 36; early social work and, 47; New Deal and, 48

social responsibility, social worker beliefs on, 74, 144–145, *147*, 149

Social Security Act, 48–49, 51–52

Social services, experience of social workers with, 2–3

social variable, intergroup dialogues and, 147

social welfare: agencies conservative ideology and, 65; benefits responsibility for, 99; centers for, 33–34; eligibility standards of, 140; federal government and, 48–50, 154; New Deal and, 48–49

social welfare organizations, political ideologies of, 98

Social Welfare Policy course, 1–2

social worker education: allowance of political ideology expression in, 104–105, 110–111, 168–170; reflective environment in, 169, 175–176; strategies for political diversity conversations in, 168–169

social work programs, perceived liberal bias of, 28–29

Social Work Reinvestment act, proposal by NASW of, 60

Social Work Speaks (National Association of Social Workers), 5, 13, 23–24, 26, 74; agenda of NASW and, 74–176; defense of positions in, 111–112; on end-of-

life care, 123; on healthcare issues, 85; in immigrants and refugees, 124–125; on issues of women, 127–128; on minimum wage, 102–103; mission statement and, 136–137; on social justice, 110, 157; social worker views on, 175–177; on welfare reform, 126

social work students, political ideology of, 77, 157–158, 167–168

social work workforce, support for, 161

socioeconomic status, value change and, 69

sociologically oriented human behavior courses, 100

Specht, H., 47

spectrum, of political ideology, 7

spiritual content in curriculum, social work faculty on, 69–70

SSI. *See* Supplemental Security Income

staff, hiring of by charity organization societies, 45

Starr, Ellen Gates, 40

state benefit eligibility, social worker views on, 115

State Children's Health Insurance Program (SCHIP), 57

status quo, conservative promotion of, 48

stereotypes, discussion of, 107, 147

strong professional identity, in study of Fisher, 65

student activism, political ideology and, 80, 154, 175–176, 181–182

supervision, of social workers, 133–134, 172–173

■ 232 ■

INDEX

supervisor: prejudice and, 158–159; questions on value conflicts, 134

supervisor-social worker relationship, political discussions and, 172

Supplemental Nutrition Assistance Program (SNAP), 125–126, 132

Supplemental Security Income (SSI), 53

supply-side economics, 54

Supreme Court, religious freedom case of, 59

sympathy, emphasis on in COS movement, 38

TANF. *See* Temporary Aid for Needy Families

tangential research, on political ideology of social workers, 72

Tax Cuts and Jobs Act, 59

teacher beliefs, social worker beliefs compared with, 66–67

technology, social good and, 165

Temporary Aid for Needy Families (TANF), 2, 56, 115, 116, 132

tenets, of political ideology, *153*

tension, between client and provider, 118–120, 131–132

third stage, of intergroup dialogues, 150

three-tier model, of social empathy, 144

Timbers, V. L., 84

Topics and Issues, with Potential Divergent Student Ideological Views, *91*

traditional activism, institutional activism contrasted with, 64

traditional values, New Right ideology on, 11–12

trained caseworkers, replacement of voluntary visitors by, 46

transformative justice, Jacobs on, 83

Trattner, W. I., 38, 39–43

Trump, Donald J., 58–59, 189; concern of NASW over, 60

Ukraine support, bipartisan support for, 190

undocumented caregiver, welfare system and, 1, 123–124, 132–133

undocumented client, differing views of students on, 93, 98, 115

unemployment, social worker views on, 145

United States (U.S.), 48, 50

universities, research on varying, 182–183

University of California at Berkeley, 28–29

University of Central Florida, 28–29

U.S. *See* United States

use, of self, 130, *131*, 134

vaccine: conservative social worker client and, 121, 159; requirements, 102–103

value based-conflicts, 96, 116–117, 128–131, 134–135

value base of social work profession, tension between political diversity and, 32, 178–179

value change, socioeconomic status and, 69

values: individual-government relationship and, 4–5; influence on practice of, 73; social work training programs and, 110–111

■ 233 ■

INDEX

Valutis, S., 108
Varley, B. K., 63, 69, 70
Veteran, NASW position on,
 166
vice president role in certification,
 bipartisan support for, 190
violence prevention, NASW position
 on, 162
volunteer visitors, of COS model,
 37–38; replacement by trained
 caseworkers of, 46–47
Voting Rights Act, 51

Wagaman, M. A., 144
Wagner, D., 64
waiting list selection, political views
 and, 134–135
Walker, R. B., 7
War on Poverty, of Johnson
 administration, 51, 52
Watkins, Julia, 30–31
wealth, as intrinsically good, 38
welfare state, lack of research on
 social worker views on, 86

welfare system, undocumented
 caregiver and, 1, 123–124, 132–133
Will, George, 27–29; response of
 social work organizations to,
 30–31
Wilmer, C. M., 70
Woodcock, R., 128–129
work experience, political beliefs
 and, 71
work requirements for
 welfare programs, Clinton
 administration and, 56
work setting, political beliefs and, 71
World War I: protest by settlement
 houses against, 45–46; support
 by charity society organizations
 of, 45–46

Yancy, G. I., 84
Yip, K., 106–107, 129–130
young child, undocumented
 caregiver and, 132–133
young social workers, views on
 racism of, 83

Printed and bound by CPI Group (UK) Ltd, Croydon, CR0 4YY

10/06/2024